PORTFOLIO

BURNOUT

Anju Jain is a senior psychologist and business leader who has worked across multinational organizations in the US and Asia. She has a PhD in developmental psychology from Pennsylvania State University and a collective work experience of over twenty years in academia, business and entrepreneurship. She is the author of *Step Up: How Women Can Perform Better for Success*.

ADVANCE PRAISE FOR THE BOOK

'Employee satisfaction is critical for building high-performance teams. A big reason for falling motivation is burnout, which can be prevented and overcome. A refreshing look by Anju Jain on how you can beat burnout and win happy times for yourself. Do read!'—Vineet Nayar, author, *Employees First, Customers Second*

'We live in a fast-paced world and burnout is one of the outcomes of this pace. Burnout happens because of unsupportive bosses or colleagues, poor team dynamics and failure to look after personal health. Anju Jain has written a timely book'—Shiv Shivakumar, group executive president, Aditya Birla Group

ANJU JAIN

burnout

beat fatigue
to thrive in an
overworked world

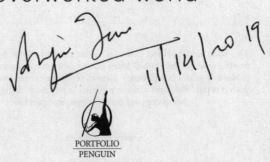

PORTFOLIO
PENGUIN

An imprint of Penguin Random House

PORTFOLIO

USA | Canada | UK | Ireland | Australia
New Zealand | India | South Africa | China

Portfolio is part of the Penguin Random House group of companies
whose addresses can be found at global.penguinrandomhouse.com

Published by Penguin Random House India Pvt. Ltd
7th Floor, Infinity Tower C, DLF Cyber City,
Gurgaon 122 002, Haryana, India

Penguin
Random House
India

First published in Portfolio by Penguin Random House India 2019

Copyright © Anju Jain 2019

All rights reserved

10 9 8 7 6 5 4 3 2 1

The views and opinions expressed in this book are the author's own and the
facts are as reported by her which have been verified to the extent possible,
and the publishers are not in any way liable for the same.

ISBN 9780143442868

Typeset in Adobe Jenson Pro by Manipal Digital Systems, Manipal
Printed at Thomson Press India Ltd, New Delhi

This book is sold subject to the condition that it shall not, by way of trade
or otherwise, be lent, resold, hired out, or otherwise circulated without the
publisher's prior consent in any form of binding or cover other than that in
which it is published and without a similar condition including this condition
being imposed on the subsequent purchaser.

www.penguin.co.in

MIX
Paper
FSC   FSC® C010615

To
Professor R.K. Jain,
Vinod Jain,
Ganesh Iyer,
Ishira and Aaina

CONTENTS

Physical Energy

Emotional Stability

Mental Focus

Make a Change

PART III: ENVIRONMENTAL STRATEGIES

PART IV: BURNOUT AMONG CHILDREN

Foreword

GLOBALIZATION, CONNECTIVITY AND competitiveness have changed the way we work, conduct business and lead our lives. While there are several positives to this new way, there are, of course, negatives too. One of them happens to be the rising rates of burnout.

A significant number of people I encounter talk about being burned out. People from all walks of life feel they are over worked, sleep-deprived and anxious, and sense they don't have balance in their lives. Left unaddressed, this will lead to regrets. The regret of broken relationships. The regret of neglected health. The regret of not being the person one always wanted to be. The cost is not only to the individual—in the long run, society pays the price.

While many talk about the challenge, few take it upon themselves to do something about it. In this compelling book, Anju breaks down a complex issue and makes it accessible through her common sense and easy-to-understand writing. She looks at the issue from the lens of the individual as well as the environment.

Throughout the course of my thirty-seven-year long career, if there is one thing I have learned, it is that you have to plan your personal life with the same rigour as your professional life. Anju echoes this. She recommends YOU—the individual—to take charge and strengthen your personal capabilities with full discipline so you are in a better position to go through the motions of life. She offers pragmatic and simple, science-backed strategies and tools to do so.

What I also like is that she calls out the role of organizations and societies in the burnout equation. She urges organizations to build humane cultures and nurture humane leaders. I can clearly see how these efforts can enhance employee engagement and well-being. As a leader, the only multiplier effect of your given talent is being able to engage the people you lead.

What makes this book relatable and an interesting read is that there are several real stories, anecdotes and fascinating research to support the claims and recommendations that Anju has put forward. It is easy to read and you will find several practical and impactful learnings as you go through it. I enjoyed reading it and it made me think about some aspects of my own life.

As a final note, and to reiterate, if you are waiting for your boss to tap you on your shoulder and say, 'We need to do something about your burnout', it will be a long wait. Your only defence is a good offence and the fact that you have picked up or downloaded this book is a good step in the right direction. Enjoy.

Cary, North Carolina
June 2019

Ed Rapp
Former group president
Caterpillar Inc.

Introduction

NOVEMBER 2016. IT is 3 p.m. A mandatory meeting of the top leadership of the company has been called. The executive committee of seven assembles in the boardroom. With a large oval teak table as the centrepiece, the room suddenly looks too cramped to accommodate everyone. What's going to be discussed is important: the resignation of the successor who was to take on the reins of the company the next quarter.

All, including the concerned executive, John, take their seats at the table. At fifty-one years of age, John has had an enviable career trajectory. His career graph has only seen upward swings. He has earned accolades for turning around failing businesses and has received the most glowing feedback from superiors, peers and teams working under him. The company has been grooming him for the last three years to take the lead.

Sitting here, John looks unusually tense and tired. His shoulders are drooping and his voice wavers as he acknowledges everyone in the room. He does not look like someone in command and ready to lead the company.

There is silence and a sense of unease in the room. The chair of the committee, Chris, opens the meeting with preliminary pleasantries and then quickly comes to the point, asking John, 'Why? Why do you want to leave when you are so close to reaching the pinnacle? Isn't this what you always wanted?'

John squirms in his chair for a second before pulling himself up and squaring his shoulders. He now appears to be more physically present and ready to talk. Gone is the droopy look. This is the John we have always seen and listened to: poised, confident and commanding everyone's attention regardless of the subject he is pontificating on.

'Chris, you know I love this company. I have given it my all, to the extent that I no longer have a life of my own. I have no choice but to exit on personal grounds,' he says.

He looks at everyone squarely. 'In the last six months, I have been out of the office seven times for high blood pressure and anxiety attacks. The doctor has asked me to take things slow before I end up with irreversible consequences. The travel, the late nights—everything is taking a toll on me. The work stress has been slowly killing me. I feel depleted and burned out. I want to get away from all this, rest a while until I get my bearings right and feel capable of working again.'

Chris and the others understand what he is saying. Everyone is privy to John's life, which hasn't been in the pink of health either physically or emotionally the last few months. On the personal front too, things don't look any better for him. There is talk going around about strains in his familial relationships.

There isn't much else to talk about.

I hear Chris ask, 'Is there anything we can do to reverse your decision? Anything at all?'

John smiles. 'Unfortunately, no, Chris. But I hope we will stay in touch and you will call me back as an adviser after I return from my year-long break with my family.'

Soon, the tension in the room is gone and everyone gets up to hug John and wish him the best for the future. The meeting adjourns after they all agree on a date for a farewell party.

Those of us lingering in the room post the meeting acknowledge that John has taken the right decision, even though it is unprecedented. He has taken stock of his life at the right time, before it could get completely out of hand. Or perhaps it is already at the breaking point, to command this extreme intervention.

And it is an extreme step in more ways than one.

An unplanned career break has a significant bearing on finances, and invites the risk of being called a failure or not being strong enough to handle the pressure. Depending on how one sees it, it is the bravest or the weakest decision any one could take.

For most people, such a decision is close to impossible because of the consequences it comes with. Not everyone has the security of finances or the mettle to call it quits. Despite the suffering, whether it is because of a work overload, misalignment with the work culture, an uncaring boss or associated stresses, the majority of people continue to be stuck in a rut. There is always the optimism and hope that things will get better one day or that this too shall pass.

IG, a senior manager in the organization, is another case in point.

IG has been in the company for over eighteen years, and is known to give his heart and soul to his work. He is an engaged and hardworking leader. I see him constantly on the run, juggling work and other commitments. Living in Asia and working closely with the organization's US office, his day begins early and ends in the wee hours the next day.

If there is one person I think who is likely to soon follow in John's footsteps, it is IG.

It wasn't too long ago that we had lunch together. It was on my insistence that he agreed to take twenty minutes off that afternoon. We hurriedly went to the cafeteria on the second floor. When I casually asked how he was doing, he placidly stated, 'I am doing well. Too much work, too little time. Everyone is trying to do more with less.'

I nodded and he continued, 'And then there are always those escalating expectations on deliverables.' You know how it is, he concluded, and dug into his meal. After a few minutes, he opened up.

Similar to other businesses, his was not performing well either, he said. Even though it was profitable, sales were not going up. 'That is still good news,' I said. He shook his head and said, 'Yes and no. Yes, the profits are there, but there is extreme pressure from the top to improve our sales numbers.' They were doing everything that was in their control. Unfortunately, there were limits. The limits of the economy itself that were impeding business opportunities.

He added that the more difficult aspect to deal with was the lack of support from his boss. The situation was being looked at in oppositional terms of 'them' and 'us'. There was no feeling of being in it together. 'Despite giving it our all, every time I have to keep defending my team, which is equally tired of this numbers game. We are the only group making profits, and yet for some reason we are being singled out and beaten up. There is no consideration or recognition of the effort we all are putting in. It is demotivating. Worse, you can't talk to anyone about it. For if you do, you would be perceived as a complainer and not strong enough to weather the storm.'

He absently played with his food and then continued in a tired voice, 'I'm not sure how long I am going to be able to pull this along. I'm hoping things will miraculously get better. But sometimes I wonder if this grind is even worth it. You know, literally killing yourself for something that doesn't give you any happiness. The only consolation I have is that at least I am paid well for the hardship I am going through. But I know I won't be able to do this for long. I want to get away from this rat race and do something more meaningful with my life.'

As I listened to him, I picked up on some key phrases:

'too much work'
'too little time'
'more with less'
'escalating expectations'
'no recognition'
'demotivating'
'hoping'
'killing yourself'
'no happiness'
'more meaningful life'

I could tell that the short lunch break was cathartic for him. He got a few moments to reflect upon his life. He seemed more determined as we walked out. Perhaps he had figured out a path that would take him to his preferred goal of a meaningful future.

But for me, it was the opposite. I felt burdened by this exchange. After John, here was another of our highfliers who was bogged down by the pressures of work, the expectations and the environment around him. It was definitely a far cry from the healthy environment we ought to be providing our people to perform in.

Not having the support of his boss and being pressured from all sides, IG was headed for a burnout. And I knew he wasn't alone in this.

Data shows that at least four in ten professionals in the US are burned out.[1] Within the health industry, five out of ten physicians[2] and seven out of ten nurses[3] are burned out. Similar is the case with school teachers, with 40–50 per cent of them dropping out within the first five years of teaching because of this very issue.

Characterized by exhaustion, low energy levels and cynicism, burnout has become the new normal: an acceptable by-product of hard work and success. The implications of burnout are grave: coronary heart disease, gastrointestinal issues, high cholesterol and even death under the age of forty-five have all been linked with it. What's worse, says Professor Mark Greenberg of Pennsylvania State University, is that even if these external signs of illness are not obvious yet, unknown to us, burnout has likely begun at the cellular level, compromising our physiological functioning and health.

On the work front, burnout results in performance and productivity challenges that cost both the individual and the organization. There is poor performance, absenteeism and attrition. Traits of collaboration, creativity and engagement are also compromised.

Apart from these, the challenges of burnout permeate personal relationships. We spend less time with our families and those who matter to us. Our over-engagement with work, and the resultant irritable and cranky disposition also don't necessarily make us the best partners to be around. We are less emotionally available and 'present' in our interactions. With the result, broken marriages, strained ties with children, and loneliness issues are common in those who fall in the burned-out category.

Given the seriousness of the issue, the obvious questions are:

- Can you beat burnout?
- Can you regulate stress?
- Can you have a great career and a wonderful family life?
- Can you regain control over your well-being?

The answer to all of the above is a resounding yes!

This book offers a comprehensive framework, which I refer to as the Well-being State Pyramid, to respond to these questions and more. It focuses on building your physical, emotional and mental capacities; these are key to not only strengthening your ability to tackle situations and lowering stress, but also ensuring you have free time and vigour to engage in things that matter. The underlying premise is that you need to be humane towards yourself—be kind and caring and don't ignore the many stress signals your body may be alerting you to. By taking timely action and proactively strengthening your whole self, you can keep burnout and its related challenges at bay.

Since we are a part of a larger ecosystem, the book also offers recommendations for our organizational and societal leaders to consider. By creating a conducive anti-burnout environment, the many triggers of burnout can be ameliorated.

Given my work experience in India, Singapore and US the last few years, the insights in here have been gleaned from individuals at these different locations. They represent varied industries and levels of organizations, from the bottom all the way to the top. Some of them admitted to being burned out while others had successfully kept burnout at bay. Together, these interactions highlight the universality and genesis of this malady along with its causes and solutions to address it.

The book is targeted at anyone who wishes to lead a burnout-free life. More importantly, it is for those who may be slowly heading towards one without even realizing it. Whether you work fifteen hours a day five to six days a week, struggle to manage work and home, or just want to be proactive about your well-being, you will find important takeaways to design your life differently.

Join me on this journey of exploration and find out how.

PART I

The Context

Some stress = Good performance

Prolonged stress = Burnout and poor
performance

Burnout is characterized by:

1) Exhaustion
2) Cynicism or indifference towards work
3) A sense of poor accomplishment

Burnout Is a Lot More than Stress

WHEN MY COLLEAGUES and friends learned that I was writing on burnout, I consistently received two kinds of responses. One: 'Wow, what a timely topic. It is much needed in today's time and age.' And two: 'I have been burned out. I would be happy to share my experiences with you.'

While I loved their willingness to come forward, their responses often threw me into a dilemma. Had they truly experienced burnout or had they gone through extreme bouts of stress? And if it was the latter, why did they think they were burned out?

For most of us, the line between stress and burnout is a blurry one. In fact, we often use the two terms interchangeably, and offhandedly too. But experts tell us that the concepts are, in fact, very different.

In its most basic form, stress is a response of the body to a situation that is perceived as a threat or challenge. Anytime we feel we are unable to cope with something, we experience stress. The dictionary defines stress as 'a state of mental or emotional strain or tension resulting from adverse or demanding circumstances'. An illness, injury, bad weather, life transitions or being late for a meeting—all these things can cause us stress. But the good part is: it is transient and finite. It ends.

Take a commonplace example. Imagine you are stuck in traffic and getting late for a meeting. You look at the throng of vehicles and your watch repeatedly. You squint your eyes, frown, squirm in your seat, look out, show your angst, perhaps mutter a few cuss words, and thump your steering wheel. The situation is clearly outweighing your ability to do anything about it. You are stressed.

Now, if you have no meeting to get to, you may not mind the traffic and not get stressed either. You may, in fact, use this time constructively: to plan your day, listen to music, or just enjoy looking at the various models of vehicles in front of you. You may think: 'Hmm, that's a nice car' or 'Those kids are driving an expensive car', or 'What is that fellow doing!' In this instance, you wouldn't view the situation as adverse or demanding. You would likely be cool and not stressed.

From these two examples, it is obvious that stress arises less from the situation and more from how we evaluate it.

Another fundamental reality about stress is that not all stress is bad. There is good stress too. Hard to believe, right? In the early 1900s, psychologists Robert Yerkes and John Dodson argued that some amount of stress is good for our performance.[1] They illustrated this through the graph below where the Y-axis measures performance and the X-axis stress. The peak of the curve in the middle indicates ideal performance and optimal stress. This is the point that signifies a sense of urgency, focus and high engagement: a state in which one can actively think, be creative and also deliver the best performance without getting overwhelmed or anxious. Contrastingly, the right end of the graph indicates extreme stress that can hinder performance. And so can being on the left side—a state of apathy—where there is neither stress nor performance.

Yerkes-Dodson Law

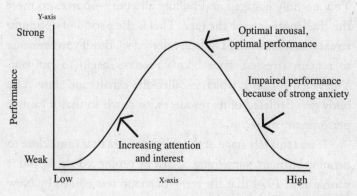

Source: https://commons.wikimedia.org/wiki/File:HebbianYerkesDodson.svg

This link between stress and performance generated so much interest that it continued to be a focus for several decades. Then, in 1956, a Canadian scientist, Hans Selye, took this concept to another level, proposing that: 'Stress is the nonspecific response of the body to any demand, whether it is caused by or results in pleasant or unpleasant conditions.'[2] He described stress as a three-stage process starting with alarm and followed by resistance and exhaustion. Collectively, he called this response the General Adaptation Syndrome.

To illustrate this, say you experience an emotionally or physically charged situation: competing in a race, for instance. In Phase 1, you get alarmed—your heart begins to pump fast and loud. You can actually hear it. You are scared and your brain signals the body to get into action. The body releases hormones that give a boost of energy. Blood is diverted to the muscles. With your resources mobilized, you are now ready to fight back. In Phase 2, you experience resistance—your temperature, blood pressure and respiration levels elevate. You are fully engaged and pulling all your resources to meet the challenge—to ace the race. This is the period of optimum stress that Yerkes and Dodson referred to. But if you continue to remain stressed, your body's reserves begin to run out. You reach Phase 3, which is called the exhaustion state. The body gets depleted of its resources, so much so that it cannot perform any more.

It was this last stage of the stress process that came close to defining burnout: something caused by prolonged stress. But it wasn't until 1974 that the term 'burnout' was coined by New York psychologist Herbert Freudenberger.[3] He characterized burnout as an overwhelming feeling of exhaustion or aggravation where both cognitive and emotional energies get depleted. Freudenberger experienced this first-hand. His own job, which was once so rewarding, was causing him fatigue and frustration. Then he observed that many of the physicians around him too had, over time, turned into depressive cynics. They increasingly treated their patients coldly and dismissively.

A similar observation was made by noted psychologist Christina Maslach, professor at the University of California, Berkeley.[4] She described burnout through three characteristics:

emotional exhaustion, cynicism and low self-efficacy. She elaborated that when exhausted, you are irritated, tired and less energetic. Cynicism happens when you become distant, cold and indifferent to others' needs, and lose empathy for people needing help. This typically occurs when passion, joy and meaning goes out of work. A sense of poor self-efficacy or lack of accomplishment sets in when there is disappointment and frustration about not being able to fulfil life plans, dreams and ambitions.

Take the case of Jessica, in her mid-forties, whose experience aligns with the above definitions of burnout. She worked in the Chicago area. She had a great family with a supportive spouse and three beautiful children whose ages ranged from college-going teen to primary school student. Professionally, she created behavioural treatment plans and therapies for teenagers and adults with special needs. Most of her patients demonstrated violent and extreme behaviours. Until about eighteen months ago, her work involved driving to their homes, which were spread across the state of Illinois.

Like my other friends, she too came forward to share her experience of burnout. I asked her my burning question: 'How do you know you were burned out and not stressed?'

With a thoughtful look, she said, 'Well, burnout stems from stress, doesn't it?' She patiently walked me through her experience.

'In the beginning my work was fun. I loved my job and the difference I was making in people's lives. I was very good at my work because of which my employer sent more and more clients my way. I didn't say no and kept on stretching myself. I was putting in a lot more than other colleagues. Over time, it all became exhausting and stressful. The long-distance driving and dealing with difficult cases started to take a toll on me. I was gaining weight and developing acute backaches. My moods were affected; I was short-tempered and impatient. My job had begun to affect my personal life. I had to get out of it. Eventually I did.'

Clearly, unlike stress, burnout is neither transient, nor conducive for optimal performance or well-being. It is equal to undergoing stress for prolonged periods of time. It has actually been compared to a dying candle, suggesting that even though once upon a time the fire burned bright, because of a lack of resources it no longer does. Work output is at the pace of a slow smoulder, unexciting and insignificant.

This was what Jessica was experiencing, and so was Travis.

Travis was a senior executive in Singapore. He confessed to being burned out two years ago. He was on a fast track, he said. At the age of thirty-two, he was a department head at a multinational company, and by thirty-eight, a vice president (VP) of product planning and development. By forty, he was promoted to a VP for the Asia region. Somewhere along the way, he got burned out.

As we talked about his brush with burnout, he said, 'When you are ambitious, you do everything to climb the ladder. You get in early to work, stay in late, work weekends, skip vacations, all the while being obsessed about your performance, promotion and future. You take great pride in your workaholism—it's like a badge of honour. As you run in the fast lane, you fleetingly notice other things around you. You feel guilty about not taking care of yourself but you ignore those signals. You appease yourself by saying you will attend to your needs once the work gets over. You fail to exercise, sleep or rest. Everything is about work, work and more work.

'When things go according to your plan—promotion, recognition, rewards, etc.—you are elated and feel you have conquered the world. But if they don't, you start becoming cynical and negative about the organization, your boss and yourself. Tiny-tiny stresses compound and take you to a point where you begin to lose interest in your work. You participate less and less. You don't want to talk to anyone. You feel empty. You burn out.'

Travis lost his motivation and drive to go on. He became cynical about his future and his effectiveness took a nosedive. It took several health issues and a bad divorce to change his perspective on work. These are classic consequences of burnout.

Burnout has a way of creeping up on you. The only silver lining is that it brings a rude awakening that forces you to finally pause and take charge of your life.

As Travis and I ended our conversation, I was reminded of Kahlil Gibran's words on work:

Work is love made visible.
    And if you cannot work with love but only with distaste, it is better that you should leave your work and sit at the gate of the temple and take alms of those who work with joy.

For if you bake bread with indifference, you bake a bitter bread that feeds but half man's hunger.

And if you grudge the crushing of the grapes, your grudge distils a poison in the wine.

And if you sing though as angels, and love not the singing, you muffle man's ears to the voices of the day and the voices of the night.[5]

Indeed, all work is empty if there is no love. Burnout reflects that empty state.

Can you now tell if you are stressed or burned out?

40 to 50 per cent of the employee
population is burned out

Age, gender and industry are no bar

Some are more prone to burnout than others

2

The Crisis: Burnout Is Everywhere

A COLLABORATIVE 2016 study led by research companies Future Workplace and Kronos Incorporated showed that 40 per cent of office workers in the United States and Canada feel burned out.[1] In other words, four out of ten people are cynical about their work, come to office tired in the morning, and are not fully 'present' when you are having important discussions with them.

Have you noticed that in a meeting? Or are *you* one of those four people?

As I stare at this statistic, I am reminded of IG, whom I introduced you to earlier. We met again a few months later. He was a different person. Gone was his passion for work, and what was left was complete disinterest. He wasn't happy with his job and was looking for a way out. Here's what he shared:

'I have lost my motivation. No matter what I do, there are some challenges in my job that I simply have no control over. The measurement criteria for the success of my business are ill defined. We can all see it, but my boss and some other stakeholders don't want to. Any change I bring in on one side of my business has a counter-effect on the other. I feel I am victimized for no fault of mine. I have tried my best, but it isn't working any more. If my team and I are not doing well, so be it. I am not going to worry about it now. I can't change my boss or others, but I can change myself.'

This is a typical response when you burn out: you become cynical, indifferent or uncaring. I recognized that IG had had enough. Not too long afterwards, he found a solution: he quit and joined another company that was more aligned to his vision and expectations.

More and more people are feeling tired and burned out. In analysing the General Social Survey of 2016, researchers Emma Seppala and Marissa King,[2] affiliated with the Yale School of Management, found that close to 50 per cent of the respondents were consistently exhausted because of work, compared with 18 per cent two decades ago. So if earlier we had two burned out people in a room of ten, that number had now increased to almost half the room.

That the incidence of burnout is increasing is also reflected in other areas. Earlier, burnout was restricted to those of a certain age and experience; today, it is very much a part of the millennial world (those born during 1980–2000) as well. A Statista research study in 2017 showed that millennials are the fastest-growing segment in the burnout space.[3] They are putting in long and incessant hours, causing them chronic stress and anxiety. A Gallup study of nearly 7500 full-time US employees showed that 28 per cent of millennials felt 'frequent or constant' burnout at work, compared with 21 per cent of workers in older generations.[4] An additional 45 per cent of millennial workers said they 'sometimes' felt burned out at work, suggesting that overall 76 per cent or seven in ten millennials experienced some level of burnout. It has been argued that this generation wants to reach the heights in a hurry. They take on too much, hold themselves to high expectations and standards, but lack appropriate coping mechanisms to deal with extreme pressures.

Nicole is one such millennial I know of. Born to Chinese parents, she is an ambitious, hard-working woman residing in Singapore. She taught my girls how to play the piano. Extremely focused and passionate about her work, she was constantly on the go, with back-to-back lessons scheduled on her calendar. During the day, she worked at a music store, and in the evenings, she was out giving private lessons. In between she would also run errands for a couple of families.

Her sole aim was to make money, quickly, and send most of it to her parents. 'My parents are farmers who worked hard all their lives. I want to make enough so I can make their life comfortable.' I wished her well when I relocated to the US eighteen months ago. Only recently I learned that she is unwell, recovering from severe exhaustion and anxiety episodes. Overwork coupled with lack of rest was responsible for her condition.

Nicole is far from being alone in this situation. With this age segment constituting a critical portion of the working population, burnout has become a significant concern for the human resource (HR) sector. The 2016 Future Workplace and Kronos Incorporated study referred to above, which surveyed over 600 HR leaders—VPs, directors, chief HR officers and managers—across different industry sectors and in companies with employee strength ranging from 100 to more than 2500, sheds light on the critical nature of this issue.[5] Data revealed that for 95 per cent of these leaders, burnout was the biggest threat to their organizations. Nearly 50 per cent of them said employee burnout was responsible for up to half of their annual workforce turnover.

Besides the corporate arena, other sectors are equally, if not more, plagued with burnout. When Maslach started her exploration on this subject in the 1970s, she found it to be significantly pervasive in the 'giving' field, such as social work, or where human interactions and emotions were involved.[6] Over the years, burnout has taken the shape of a crisis in the health industry. A 2011 survey conducted by the Mayo Clinic and the American Medical Association showed that 45 per cent of physicians showed signs of burnout.[7] When the survey was repeated three years later, the rate had increased by a whopping 9 points to 54 per cent.

These escalating rates are not only a cause for concern for the physicians themselves, but also for the patients who are being attended by these very exhausted caregivers. Being operated on by a surgeon who may be burned out—exhausted, unfocused and prone to making errors—is a scary proposition. Not a good space or hands to be in!

To understand the gravity of the situation, I spoke with Dr Tony Avellino, former CEO of the OSF HealthCare

Neurological Institute in Peoria, Illinois. He shared some realities of this profession: 'Physician burnout is very common. You are overworked, exhausted, sleep deprived, and constantly on the go. There is no time to take a break so you can recoup or recharge yourself. Besides seeing patients, there are bureaucratic processes and pressures to bring in revenue for the hospital. There are performance markers tied to how many patients you see in a month. You feel the pressure and stress. Some physicians are impacted more severely than others; there are anxiety attacks, depression and suicidal episodes. What is worse, though, is that you are unable to talk to anyone about this. You fear being seen as a failure. So you keep it inside you and that continues to fester and gnaw at you. Sooner or later that chronic stress leads to a burnout.'

Dr Michel Kliot, a clinical professor of neurosurgery at the Stanford University School of Medicine, elaborated on the bureaucracy that Tony alluded to. 'There is so much more to do today than just seeing and treating your patients that generates additional stress. As medical overheads rapidly and significantly increase, physicians are pressured to contribute to the bottom line of the hospital by seeing and operating on more patients while abiding by an ever-increasing number of new health regulations that are quite burdensome. In addition, one has to use an electronic medical record that is frequently updated and can be quite challenging and time-consuming. Although it offers some advantages, it infringes upon valuable time spent conversing with and evaluating patients. This can make the visit less beneficial and worthwhile both to the patient and the treating physician. These changes are all contributing to decreased patient satisfaction and increased physician burnout.'

If physicians are facing the heat, nurses aren't behind either. We all know the kind of work they do. It's tough to be on your feet all the time dealing with suffering patients. Not surprisingly, seven out of ten nurses in the US feel burned out.[8] Moreover, their depression rate is at 18 per cent compared to the general national prevalence of 9 per cent.

A friend of mine, Jennifer, is a registered nurse at a hospital in Virginia. About her profession, she shared: 'Being a healthcare giver is mentally exhausting. It is cumulative and requires a very strong support system to balance out the stress of it. You are dealing not only with patients, but their families as well. Supporting them, especially after they receive bad news, is extremely hard. You feel their pain, but you simply cannot show it. You bottle it up and keep it inside you. Over time, that takes a toll on you—physically, emotionally and even mentally. I still dream about some of the patients I have lost over the years.'

Long work hours, heavy workload, dealing with matters of life and death, lack of rest, and managing organizational demands have a serious impact on the health and well-being of physicians and nurses. In turn, this has strong implications for the kind of care they give to their patients.

But burnout doesn't stop at these professions. Our children are being taught by teachers who are exhausted, cynical or performing well below their capacities. For example, nearly half of the teachers in India have been shown to suffer from burnout.[9] A 2014 Education Staff Health Survey indicated 91 per cent of school teachers in the UK had experienced stress in the previous two years.[10] The US was no exception. More than 41 per cent of teachers left the profession within five years of joining because of burnout.[11]

Kavita, who was a primary school teacher in a government school in New Delhi, left her job at the age of forty-three as she was burned out. She attributed her departure to lack of autonomy and bureaucratic control. 'You had to teach from an examination point of view. That was extremely restrictive. You couldn't really share your knowledge or pass on to children the joy of learning. It was frustrating. Also, there were too many demands—constant need for data, audits, applying for grants, etc.—for which we were neither trained nor had the infrastructure in place. Of course, we missed deadlines in our submissions. It was just too much stress that I couldn't deal with any more. I was getting burned out.'

Fast-forward to almost three decades later when Shikha, an elementary school teacher in another part of the world, the US, recently shared her routine, the work-related challenges, and how they impacted her sanity. It didn't appear that her experience and Kavita's were any different, despite the gap of three decades between them.

According to Shikha, 'The work pressures are severe. Both from the school and the self. The combined expectations make you slog. You want to do well for yourself, for the children you are responsible for, and also build a good name for your school. Unfortunately, the budget and resource challenges take a toll on you. You work like a machine, do more with less. On top of that, there are other challenges to navigate every day: politics, lack of flexibility and control, disgruntled parents and many other roadblocks that are just not under your control. They fester and the pot gets so full that you burn out.'

A question that often comes up is whether burnout is a gendered issue. Is one gender more prone to burnout than the other? If you look at the data, especially from the health sector, it shows women surgeons more prone to burnout than men.[12] This rate of burnout varies anywhere within 43–45 per cent for women and 37–39 per cent for men. The 2018 Medscape report attributes this variance to greater work expectations and work–home conflicts among women.

Research led by Dr Nancy Beauregard from Montreal University corroborated the above observation.[13] Her findings were based on 2000 employees she followed over the course of four years and across multiple workplaces. The gender difference was attributed to the different working conditions men and women were subjected to. She found that because women are less likely to be given positions of power, it increases their frustration. To handle that, they use household chores as a strategy to 'vent'. Although this can be a buffering mechanism against burnout if used temporarily, it can lead to problems in the long term. The strategy 'can become a trap and result in missed opportunities for advancement, causing women to remain confined to positions with low decision-latitude'. Inevitably, this feeds into the cycle of burnout.

Take the case of Neha, who is in her early thirties and working as an engineering professional in Chennai, India. The mother of a two-year-old, she was highly committed to her work. During one of our conversations, she shared her dilemma: 'I want to do good work and move up the ladder, but I don't see enough opportunities. I often end up doing the "softer" projects whereas the guys in my team get the high-visibility ones. It is demotivating. It suggests that I am not capable or smart enough. I have talked to my boss, but I don't see any change happening. Sometimes I wonder if this kind of work is even worth leaving my child in daycare for. This trade-off doesn't make any sense. Perhaps I should just quit and at least enjoy being with him.'

This is the kind of frustration Dr Beauregard referred to. It indicates just how demoralizing it can be for women when roadblocks surface in their careers, when they are unable to leverage their skills or be excited about what they do. Pad this with their other responsibilities and conflicts, and we have a perfect recipe not just for burnout but also attrition, which isn't bad just for women—it's bad for companies too.

From the above, it is obvious that burnout is pervasive across the board, irrespective of industry, age or gender.

But on one issue, there is still plenty of ongoing debate. What causes burnout? Is it the individual or the environment? Or is it a mix of both?

More work ≠ More success

Burnout is a result of:

1) Societal Expectations
2) Organizational Cultures
3) Individual Choices

3

Why Burnout Is Out of Control

KEVIN, WHO I have known for several years and who was my boss at one time, maintains that he has never been burned out. Despite the long days he put in, you would always find him upbeat and ready to take on more challenges. I had never heard him say he was tired, overly stressed or in need of a break. On the contrary, he was always full of energy and positivity.

Not necessarily an ideal role model in terms of the number of hours he worked, but for sure an inspiring one in terms of keeping spirits high. When I asked him how he managed this, he said, 'You just have to figure it out. I have clearly defined priorities—I have delegates I completely trust, and I make sure I take time away from work to recharge so I am not consumed with work to the exclusion of all else. When I feel like I am on the edge, I take a couple of days off. You have to unplug to keep yourself sane or engage in some distracting activities to remove stress from your life.'

Undoubtedly, the proclivity to burn out rests on several factors. Your individual characteristics—personality, threshold for pressure and ability to regulate emotions—all these can push you towards or shield you from the negative impacts of too much or incessant work.

The environment plays a huge role as well. Factors such as the nature of your job, the team you are part of, the support of your boss, and many other variables can have a substantial say on the outcome.

One of the great philosophers of all time, Augustine, talked about this nature–nurture interaction.[1] He reinforced the concept of free will, whereby, as individuals, we have freedom or free will, but it is constrained by the choices our environment offers us. In other words, we have the autonomy to do what we want, but that can only transpire within the perimeter of options available to us.

Relating this philosophy to Kevin's case, it would be fair to say that he had both internal and external factors working in his favour. He was driven and motivated, but he also had the support of his team, boss and organization to help him through his challenges. He was able to leverage them to his benefit. Now imagine if he didn't have those resources or a support system. His free will may have been limited. He may have not been as engaged or driven and likely frustrated.

Given this bi-directional interaction, burnout is a result of both individual and environmental variances.

The cultural influence

Some say we are a product of our culture. Others say culture is an outcome of our collective behaviour. Both are right in their own ways. Subsistence patterns and economies at a point in time set the ball rolling for what was expected and what wasn't.

In earlier days, survival was all about existence: safety, food and shelter. All our efforts were focused on that. We worked hard to make ends meet. While this remains a fundamental truth, there are many people who have taken survival to a different level. There is a constant desire to push yourself, do better than yesterday. For many, in a professional context, survival is aligned with the following terms:

- Achievement
- Position
- Power
- Titles
- Happiness
- Money
- Fame
- Friendships
- Strength
- Purpose
- Busyness

Those who possess these attributes survive and also inadvertently define the modern success idol. We have internalized the notion that hard and non-stop work, even at a personal cost, are acceptable in order to succeed. By the same token, idleness is a disgrace and only effort spent on work is to be rewarded.

'When culture and societal forces lay emphasis on hard work and productivity, then stress, pressure and burnout become acceptable ways of life. So much so that one doesn't find anything amiss or wrong with the situation,' says Marshall Goldsmith, a well-known leadership coach and author.

Like any cultural norm, our belief in this work ethic is principally influenced by socialization experiences during childhood and adolescence. From day one, perhaps even earlier, we are socialized to such cultural prescriptions. We are exposed to a whole slew of 'right' stimuli so we can develop into that perfect being who can navigate and survive in this world. When in the womb, our mothers eat right, rest, expose us to Beethoven's music, keep us away from negativity, and do whatever they can to give us the best start for success in life. This continues as we enter the world: more exposure to Beethoven, Mozart, Little Einsteins, interactive toys and stimulating books.

You would agree that every interaction is a calculated one: to make us smart, analytical, intelligent and everything else that society cherishes. Our schools, colleges and workplaces nurture and value these very qualities. They reinforce the value of hard work and the associated rewards in the form of grades or deliverables. According to Dr Jeff Devens, a counsellor and school psychologist working at the Singapore American School, 'This push and pull is mutual. Children are stretching beyond limits to get the best education there is. They are working hard to distinguish themselves from the rest. Likewise, colleges and workplaces are also expecting high-achieving students and employees, respectively.'

It has been almost over two years since I saw my colleague Asha driving herself crazy. Her son, a tenth-grader, was an average student at the Singapore American School. More out of concern about what people would say if he didn't score good marks or get into a 'good' college, Asha was pushing him to work harder. She was frantically signing him up for tuitions and extra support classes. Her logic was: 'Unless you push them, they don't shine. I am doing this for his future. Tomorrow, he has to compete with all kinds of kids—he'd better be prepared for that.'

While well intentioned, Asha, and parents in general, are stressing themselves and their children to align with societal expectations. We all have come to view stress as a normal part of life, childhood included. At one point or the other, we have asked our children, 'Aren't you stressed about your exam tomorrow?' or 'I don't see the fire in you, think you will ace it?' or 'Can you please get to work and not waste your time?' The underlying message in all this is: 'Work harder!' Unless we see them buried in their books, sleep-deprived or 'suffering', we don't believe they are working hard enough. Not surprisingly, children are as prone to burnout as adults are.

There is no doubt that we are an achievement-oriented society, leading a life of competition. We believe hard, incessant work, sweat and tears are the only way to succeed and be happy. Our belief in 'can-do', 'everything is possible', 'nothing is impossible' and 'if you try hard, you will succeed' pushes us to keep going and not give up. The more effort we put in, the better the results will be.

We support the linear formula of more work = more success.

But this is where the problem lies. Not all hard work, especially without rest and recovery, leads to success.

Arguably, it also depends on what qualifies as success to begin with.

Dr Derek, a physician in Illinois, illustrates this point. He told me, 'My burnout started in high school. Like others, I was under tremendous pressure to get good grades. I was stressed and anxious, but I was told to ignore it and continue slogging. I did that. Then I entered medical school. There again, life was the same, with no breather. As a practising doctor, things didn't get any better. Long hours and exhaustion coupled with genuine mistakes only exacerbated my stress levels. Silently, I battled my fears to establish my credibility. But in the process, my performance declined and the pressure of that led to my burnout.'

Hard work doesn't always pan out favourably.

In reality, more work ≠ more success.

Some 2000 years ago, the Roman philosopher Lucius Seneca informed people about the dangers of non-stop work: 'Just as you must not force fertile farmland as uninterrupted productivity will soon exhaust it, so too will the constant effort sap our mental vigour.' Wisely, he recommended short periods of rest and relaxation to restore our powers. 'Our minds must relax: they will rise better and keener after a rest.'[2]

Culture sets the boundaries for us to perform for both the good and the bad. Non-stop work and the resulting stress, with the ultimate aim of accumulating power and wealth, have become the hallmarks for success. We measure a country's progress by its GDP, a company's success by its revenues. Those who make it to the Forbes list of the most influential people do so because of the wealth and titles they have accumulated. Given this constant reinforcement of what success looks like, it isn't surprising that we have become work-obsessed, despite the fact that it comes with burnout.

Macro trends

While the above expectations constitute one part of the issue, there are other trends simultaneously augmenting the impact. Globalization, competitiveness and incessant connectivity have transformed the nature of how we work and live. These new trends, along with the winds of outsourcing, artificial intelligence and talent availability have brought additional challenges. Responsibilities have increased with the expectation of 'do more with less', and reliance on collaboration, teamwork and intense second-to-second communication has become the norm. There is greater insecurity, fear of losing jobs, and pressure to outperform each other.

A 2009 study by Leslie Perlow and Jessica Porter of Harvard Business School found that 94 per cent of Americans in professional services (consultants, accountants, investment bankers, lawyers, IT employees and the like) worked more than fifty hours; almost all of them said they put in sixty-five or more hours per week.[3] Mind you, these numbers don't include the twenty to twenty-five hours a week most of them spent working outside the office.

A separate study conducted by the Manpower Group—a world leader in innovative workforce solutions—showed the distribution of work hours by country.[4] Relative to the stipulated forty hours a week, the maximum number of hours were clocked by Indian millennials at fifty-two hours a week, followed by China's forty-eight, the US's forty-five and the UK's forty-one hours. Though these numbers vary from Perlow's study cited above because of different research designs, suffice it to say that work hours are simply getting extended. Workers are giving up their vacation time to be in office. In 2018, more than half of Americans (52 per cent) left their vacation days unused for fear of returning to a pile of work, having no one to cover for them when away, experiencing lack of support from the boss or the risk of appearing less dedicated to their careers.[5]

The breakdown of the family structure and changing role divisions have also left us vulnerable. With the increasing number of women at work and the prevalence of single and divorced families, work pressures and other demands have gone up significantly. For example, in one study, Professor Lieke Brummelhuis and colleagues from Utrecht University in the Netherlands linked the presence of young children and increasing household chores to burnout.[6] Taking care of young children can be overwhelming, leaving little room for parents to attend to themselves. The struggle to balance the demands of work, family and more, without outside assistance, can easily lead to a sense of overwhelm, stress, and if not controlled, to burnout, according to the research team.

Take the case of Raj, a new father working as an accountant in a local Bengaluru company. 'I'm tired most of the time,' he said. 'When my wife, Prema, had to go back to work to help with family finances, I had to take on more responsibility at home. By the time we both get home from work, take care of the child and do household chores, we are both so done and exhausted. We wake up tired the next morning, and it's the same thing all over again. It is super hard to manage it all.'

Aside from childcare, as life spans lengthen, care of the elderly too has become a growing area of responsibility for many families. Dealing with an elderly person's physical, emotional and psychological ailments can be a physical and emotional drain on personal resources.

Here's an example shared by a colleague. It's Wednesday night, and Shilpi and Pankaj have just got home from picking up the kids from archery lessons after stopping by at the grocery store. They are running through the evening to-do list: the dog needs to be walked, the laundry folded, dinner made, homework checked and a work presentation done. Shilpi turns on the oven and that's when her mother calls. Her asthma is bothering her again, can Shilpi take her to the doctor? Shilpi instantly says yes. When she hangs up, she closes her eyes for a moment, rearranging her evening schedule in her head. She takes a deep breath and asks Pankaj to take care of some things at home. But some tasks would have to be tackled by her the next day, adding to her already packed Thursday schedule.

Externally, country policies and legislations are also adding their own twists to the situation. While well intentioned, some have become a cause of increasing work pressures. For example, the implementation of the Electronic Health Record (EHR) system as a regulatory mandate is seen as the biggest cause for physician burnout.

Dr Christine Sinsky, the VP of professional satisfaction at the American Medical Association, and her colleagues found that physicians in the US spent only 27 per cent of their time interacting directly with patients and the rest on EHR data entry and desk work.[7] They contended that time spent in meaningful interactions with patients used to be a powerful driver of physician career satisfaction, but with increased paperwork and time on the computer, that is no longer the case. More and more physician burnout is being attributed to this peripheral work. According to Dr Tait Shanafelt, who promotes physician well-being as a chief wellness officer at Stanford University, EHR has led to 'a number of unintended negative consequences including reducing efficiency, increasing clerical burden and increasing the risk of physician burnout'.[8]

Teacher burnout too is being attributed to bureaucracy and regulations. Shikha, the public school teacher I talked about earlier, remarked, 'Instead of focusing our energies on teaching children, we are more worried about top-down administrative stuff. We are spread so thin that it isn't even practical to do everything any more. Because something has to give to accommodate more demands, our teaching suffers. And when that happens, we don't feel good, get stressed and try to play a catch-up game to recover the lost time.'

For that matter, rampant technological upgrades and highly improved connectivity on our fingertips have also fuelled the challenge. With our ability to work anytime from anywhere, the boundaries between home and work have disappeared. Out of habit, we spend more time working than enjoying personal or quiet time.

Together, these environmental forces have redefined the very nature of work and how we go about doing it.

The organizational factors

Time and again, research has shown that burnout arises within the context of our workplaces. When we join a new company or take on a different role, we are excited, engaged and motivated to perform. However, long hours, pressures of deadlines or frustrating interpersonal interactions, combined with personal demands, slowly drive us to burnout.

Recall the case of IG? He was engaged to begin with but soon got frustrated and stressed with his work and the related interpersonal dynamics. Classified as 'at-risk' for burnout, he eventually burned out and left the company.

According to Christina Maslach, burnout is triggered by the following factors:[9]

- Work overload (too much to do)
- Lack of control (discretion or say in what you do)
- Insufficient rewards (feedback or recognition)
- Community breakdown (belongingness, support)
- Unfairness (respect)
- Conflicting values (meaning)

She emphasized that when there is a mismatch among one or more of these areas, burnout can be a likely outcome.

Mike, a long-time executive at Xerox Corporation, attributed his burnout to conflicting values and a lack of trust in the leadership. He said, 'There was a time when we were going through a tough patch: reorganizations, cost-cutting and lay-offs. There was tremendous pressure to deliver and also save our jobs. The morale of the company was low. But the executives who were driving this mandate were protecting themselves and their people. They talked about cost-cutting, yet they got their bonuses. They talked about lay-offs, yet they were keeping their people safe. Personally, this was very disturbing.

'As a good manager, to keep my employees engaged, I doubled my communication efforts. That meant being on and available for all time zones. It was taxing. Further, when my employees questioned the leadership's behaviour, I had no answers for them. They were reading it right and there was no way I could contradict their assessments. As a coping mechanism and to process my frustrations and stress, I began to hang out with my colleagues after work and drank excessively. I would go home late and that started to impact my family life. I was preoccupied, distant and not fully present at home. I vividly recall the image of my then-ten-year-old daughter who would just stare at me and not utter a word. The environment at home was getting more tense as my stress at work mounted. Having had enough, my wife asked me to leave my job. She could see what it was doing to me and the family. I left Xerox. It took a while but I began to realize that a whole new world existed outside this poorly managed and dying company.'

While misplaced trust in the organization is one reason for burnout, there are others too. A 2017 study conducted by Kronos Incorporated found unfair compensation, unreasonable workload and after-hours work to be three key contributors to burnout.[10] The participants attributed their work overburden to poor management, lack of connect with the corporate strategy, and negative workplace culture.

In line with this research, Ganesh, who was an executive at Caterpillar for many years and is now the CEO of Etnyre International, a Midwest manufacturing company involved in road preservation, said, 'A leadership that focuses only on the bottom line, with no concern for "how" the job gets done, is a breeding ground for burnout. Because of the numbers mindset, there is work overload along with politics and back-stabbing which obviously don't make a healthy mix for a safe workplace. And when you don't feel safe, you are constantly on the edge. You are worried, anxious and fearful. These, coupled with bureaucracy, excessive control and lack of support, lead to poor morale and burnout.'

When leaders set the tone and demonstrate behaviours that are not conducive to employee well-being, then everything in the organization—from policies and practices to rewards and recognition—get aligned with those ill behaviours. Burnout becomes common and routine in those workplaces.

You are to blame

Though the environment plays a critical role in the genesis of burnout, so do our individual characteristics. Our personalities, drives, ambitions, needs and choices also have a say in how we feel and behave.

It was in 1990 that I met Betsy Manlove, a fellow graduate student at Pennsylvania State University. Two years ahead of me, she was doing her doctoral dissertation on identifying burnout triggers among childcare workers in rural Pennsylvania. For this, she studied a sample of 170 female childcare workers and found that all factors, individual and environmental—personality, job demands, job satisfaction, role ambiguity, role conflict, etc.—contributed to burnout.[11] Workers who exhibited negative emotions, who were over-responsive, highly reactive and had low thresholds for emotional reactions, even when faced with minor stressors, were more prone to burnout than others who showed fewer of these characteristics.

Similarly, researchers Gene Alarcon, Kevin Eschleman and Nathan Bowling from Dayton, Ohio,[12] analysed several studies and found that personality was consistently related to the three dimensions of burnout. Specifically, those who were less anxious, outgoing, responsible, cooperative, caring and demonstrated positive emotions inclusive of happiness and excitement fared low on the burnout dimensions.

No surprises here, because personality does influence our perception of the work environment. For instance, extraverts not only view a situation positively, but also evoke pleasant responses from others. Similarly, highly conscientious people evoke positive responses from their supervisors and others. So do caring and kind people; they see the positives and are treated kindly in return. This is not to say that these people don't get burned out at all. They do, when confronted by what they perceive as challenges.

An underlying trait among some individuals is their need for risk, excitement or arousal. Those looking for high levels of arousal might be drawn to high-excitement behaviours (river rafting or mountain climbing), while others may be satisfied with less exciting or risky activities (going for a walk). The choices we make evoke different levels of stress in us. Ayala Pines at Ben Gurion University in Israel emphasizes that individuals who are highly driven are at a higher risk of burnout.[13] One has to be 'on fire' to burn out; people who are not on fire—who are not highly motivated—do not burn out. This makes people with high ambitions and over-commitment streaks more susceptible, she asserted.

Tied to the 'fire' attribute, Type A personalities—characterized by competitiveness, drive, perfectionism and dependence on external rewards—are equally likely to burn out. Their excessive ambition and desire to prove themselves turn into a compulsion. They must show their colleagues—and above all, themselves—that they are doing an excellent job in every which way.

A study by Kenneth Nowack at the University of California substantiated this link. It looked at the effects of Type A behaviour on health outcomes in the face of daily life stress in a sample of forty-six employees at the UCLA Medical Centre.[14] He found that Type A behaviour directly affects both job burnout and psychological distress. To meet high personal expectations, Type A individuals take on more work. They become obsessed with handling everything themselves, which in turn bolsters their belief that they are irreplaceable. The more they work, the more resources and energy they expend, and the more easily they burn out.

Vivian, a talent acquisition professional in the US, was an obsessed high achiever. A self-proclaimed Type A person, she wanted to be a leader at the age of twenty. 'Growing up, I took on more and more as I had this goal to achieve,' she told me when we met for lunch one day. True to her vision, she continued climbing the organizational hierarchy. But underneath all that achievement were exhaustion, impatience, irritability and poor tolerance for even the minutest of imperfections. 'I used to get so annoyed that I would argue with my team and others at every turn. I wanted them to deliver exactly as per my expectations. Because of how ineffective I was becoming, I was asked to seek help from my company's employee assistance programme. After several conversations with a psychologist, I was advised to take a complete break from work. And that helped. I understood the root cause of my behaviour. I had to slow down and give breathing space to myself and others around me.'

How we regulate our emotions has also been an area of study for scholars. In 2017, a team of researchers from Florida State University and the Illinois Institute of Technology studied this link.[15] They conducted two studies to explore the relationships between emotional regulation (ER) strategies (reappraisal, suppression), school burnout and academic outcomes (grade point average or GPA, absenteeism). They defined reappraisal as changing the way a situation is conceptualized. That change can help decrease the emotional impact of the situation/stressor. For example, rather than focusing on potential mistakes while making a presentation, an individual may theorize it as a learning experience to reduce his or her anxiety. Suppression, in contrast, consists of holding back outward signs of inner feelings and is believed to be maladaptive as it fails to lessen the emotional experience. Fighting back tears after receiving a poor grade is an example of suppressing inner feelings.

In Study 1, they found that the positive aspects of reappraisal and the negative aspects of suppression were related to academic outcomes through school burnout. To establish the direction of these effects, Study 2 found that reappraisal at Time 1 negatively predicted school burnout at Time 2. Likewise, suppression of stress at Time 1 positively predicted burnout at Time 2. It was also related to lower GPA and increased absenteeism.

Together, the results underscored the fact that those who suppress stress are more prone to burnout compared to those who reappraise or analyse it.

Apart from our individual dispositions, work habits and lifestyle choices also play a critical role in our proclivity to burn out. When our schedules leave us with no time except for work, we dismiss other necessities such as sleeping, eating, exercising and socializing as unimportant. We justify these sacrifices as proof of our heroic performance at work. However, from here on, it's just a matter of time before the body comes to a grinding halt.

Researchers Kenneth Nowack and Annette Pentkowski reported that women who practise poor lifestyle habits, including drinking, smoking and unhealthy eating, exhibit a greater risk of burnout than others.[16] Mary Söderström and colleagues from Stockholm attributed 'too little sleep (less than six hours)', preoccupation with thoughts of work during leisure time, and high work demands as risk factors for burnout.[17]

Closer home, Rahul, a supply chain manager at a manufacturing plant in Chennai, illustrates this link between lifestyle and burnout. By the very nature of his job, he had to be constantly on top of things to ensure timely delivery of products. Added to that were resources shortage, system changes and upgrades, and working with teams back in the US. His dishevelled appearance, excessive smoking and zombie-like demeanour reflected this turmoil. He had no time to eat, sleep or even take a short break. He was burned out and 'losing it', as one of his team members described it.

On the other side of the spectrum is the recently retired group president of Caterpillar Inc., Ed Rapp. Responsible for over 20 per cent of Caterpillar's global revenues, he maintained that he had never been burned out despite the expanse of his responsibilities, and the travel and stress that are an inevitable part of these kinds of jobs. Ed attributed his well-being to a good, balanced lifestyle. 'I believe in being a corporate athlete. You have to focus on both body and mind fitness. Exercising daily, eating healthy and choosing the kind of day I want have kept me going,' he said.

It is obvious that both nature and nurture play a critical role in the genesis of burnout. Our individual personalities, lifestyles, personal choices, and cultural and organizational expectations interact to cause burnout. But regardless of the source, this malady comes with significant consequences for individuals and others around them.

Cost of Burnout:

1) Health
2) Relationships
3) Performance
4) Finances

4

What Happens If You
Don't Act Now

EVERY ACTION HAS an equal and opposite reaction,
Isaac Newton claimed. Burnout is no different.

Emily is a twenty-nine-year-old professional
working for a Big Four accounting firm in Singapore. We were
introduced at a seminar and hit it off instantly. A few weeks
later we met for lunch at one of her favourite places, California
Pizza Kitchen on Orchard Road. As we waited for our food
to arrive, she revealed that she was just emerging from a state
of depression caused by a long bout of burnout that started
over eighteen months ago. She was still paying the price for it,
personally and professionally.

Asian by heritage, she grew up with a tight focus on
achievements. As a child, it was drilled into her that being at
the top in academics and other activities was her sole aim in
life. Falling behind would not be tolerated by her parents, or

society for that matter. As a result, hard work and focus were an integral part of her repertoire early on.

On the family front, she had a sister who was as competitive; this often created a rift between the two when one did better than the other. Her sister was loved by all because she was an extrovert, unlike Emily, who saw herself as an introvert. From that angle, Emily felt neglected and channelled all her energy towards achieving success.

At work, she quickly rose to a managerial role and began consulting on projects related to talent and change management in the region. She thrived on challenges and aimed for good ratings, bonuses and stretch assignments as markers of success.

'I had the energy and passion for my work, so I never felt tired. Every day, my work started at 9 a.m. and ended at 10 p.m., sometimes stretching to 4 a.m. the next day. I didn't mind as I loved my work. I felt privileged that I was entrusted with high-profile projects that got me accolades from my clients. However, a year into this, I realized things were not going well for me. There were politics, unreasonable demands and limited resources that began to impact my work and mind.

'My boss was pressurizing me to take ownership of a decision I didn't make. Why should I be held accountable for something that was a team decision to begin with? People started making negative comments about me. I began to lose trust in my boss and became emotional about everything around me. My morale dropped, which affected my spirit and motivation. I felt insecure. I couldn't accept the stress. Physically, I was falling sick every month. I had never taken so many medicines or sick leave before. I was also diagnosed with muscle degeneration because of the long hours I was putting in, and also due to lack of exercise. I underwent physiotherapy for about fifteen weeks. On the work front, I was taking longer to finish tasks. My efficiency was going down. Emotionally, I was a wreck. I was depressed and lonely. I didn't want to meet anyone, and just wanted to be with myself and my pain.

'Spending long hours at work meant no life outside. I was twenty-seven, and wasn't in any relationship yet. I had no one to call a friend either. Staying away from home had widened the rift between me and my family. I continued battling with my issues for about eight months. I knew I was falling into a dark space. Then one of my colleagues at work sought me out and talked to me. I broke down and recognized what was happening to me. I had to get out of this mess. I resigned and took a six-month break.'

This episode was eighteen months ago, but Emily is still working hard to come out of it—physically, emotionally and mentally. With a hard lesson learned, she changed her approach towards work and life to prevent a repeat. She now values life more than work. She is careful about the load she takes on and has learned to say no. Instead of working insane hours, she makes it a point to close shop at a decent hour. Getting into fitness routines and keeping away from negative relationships at work and home, she is doing her best to take control of her life. Very intentionally, she has joined forums for singles and is striving to make friends. 'I am seeking a balance in life. My health and well-being are my priorities now.'

Individual costs

From Emily's example, it is obvious that the impact of burnout is felt across all domains of life. It affects the whole person—physically, emotionally and mentally.

Though not overtly noticeable, it alters the neuroendocrine systems, leading to distinct changes in the anatomy and functioning of the brain. Fascinating research from a team of scientists in Sweden shows how burnout alters neural circuits. Led by Ivanka Savic, a neurologist in the department of women and children health at the Karolinska Institutet, the team compared a group of burned-out people with a non-burned-out group.[1] They found significant physiological differences between the two groups. In the burned-out sample, the frontal cortex, which is essential for cognitive functioning, showed more pronounced thinning. The normal effects of ageing were also more prominent and there was a significant reduction in the grey matter volume associated with declining memory, language and general intelligence. The other group was measurably healthier.

Beyond the internal and not-so-readily visible physiological alterations, there are many physical signs of burnout. Since severe exhaustion is one of the defining characteristics, poor health is but an obvious outcome. A team of cross-country researchers from South Korea and the US undertook a longitudinal study of social workers.[2] They surveyed 406 California-registered social workers annually over a three-year period. The results showed that social workers with higher initial levels of burnout later reported more physical health complaints (lack of appetite, sleep disturbances, headaches and gastrointestinal infections). These outcomes were attributed to heavy demands and lack of sufficient resources in this line of work. Both overwork and emotional depletion led to heightened stress levels, and therefore poor immune functioning.

Frank, one of the leaders in my company in Singapore, once shared a glimpse of a typical workday. Holding global responsibilities for a major product line, he had his days and nights full supporting his teams in different parts of the world. Even before his day's work ended, he would be sucked into evening and nightly calls. 'Every night after a hurried dinner, I get into meetings with my boss, peers and other stakeholders in the US. Those interactions are extremely stressful; they aren't the kind where I can simply mute my phone and tune out. I have to be as alert as a hawk, for the decisions made can significantly impact my business and teams here. At the level that I am, there are politics and power games. If you don't watch out, you can easily be written off. With that stress hanging over your head, you don't have any appetite anyway. When you are stressed before, during and after meals, there are bound to be health consequences. I have had my share. I have developed severe acidity and gastrointestinal issues because of doing this daily for the last eight years.'

Prolonged stress or burnout has also been linked with coronary heart disease (CHD). It has been found to increase the risk of CHD by 1.4 times. Sharon Toker and her colleagues from the Faculty of Management, Tel Aviv University, found this in a study that looked at a sample of about 9000 working men and women in Israel.[3] Besides the increased risk, they also found that for the 20 per cent who most identified with the symptoms of burnout, that risk increased by a massive 79 per cent.

Clearly, burnout increases our vulnerability to disease and illnesses. These in turn preclude us from effective performance at work and home.

Family in the wraps

Apart from the above, there are other spillover effects. Relationships become strained. For the majority, work, meetings and incessant travel prevent them from spending any time, let alone quality time, with their families. Their irritable disposition, cynicism and negativity don't necessarily make them the best companions to be with either. So even when they are around, they are not in the best of spirits to engage or be 'present' with the family.

The spouse of a burned-out corporate leader once told me, 'My children and I have to be constantly on guard when my husband comes home in the evening. There is so much tension in the house; the kids and I are quiet and try to tiptoe around to avoid making any noise lest he gets disturbed in his meetings that typically run the whole evening. When we ask him to have dinner or go out with us, he says we should be supportive of his situation rather than place more demands on him. I have often asked myself, why are we even living together?'

Furthermore, when one partner is burned out, the other partner tries to compensate for that withdrawal from family life or neglectful behaviour towards children. Take the case of

Frank whom I've mentioned above. Given his schedule, his spouse, Anne, herself a working professional, had to step up. Single-handedly, she was carrying the responsibility of parenting. Fully understanding of Frank's situation, she was the buffer between him and their high-school children. She remarked, 'It is not easy to raise children on your own, especially when you know you could potentially share the burden with your spouse. I had to come to terms with my situation and embrace this reality early on.'

In such situations, marital discord, broken marriages and strained ties with children can become common residuals. Srinika Jayaratne, professor of social work at the University of Michigan, and colleagues looked at a set of seventy-five American child welfare workers and their husbands to assess the impact of burnout on family relations.[4] They found that those who scored high on the burnout scale reported less satisfaction with their marriages. They also reported more depression, anxiety and irritable behaviour. Consistent results were reported by Susan Jackson and Christina Maslach when they studied police couples.[5] The officers' spouses reported unsatisfactory marriages. After work, the police officers spent their time away from the family, usually drinking.

Travis, the Singapore executive who had experienced burnout, recalled, 'You get so entangled in your own life that you are not even aware of what you are doing. You don't take your spouse out for dinner or a drink; instead you go to the business lounge and drink alone. You don't take vacations with your family because you have teleconferences and you worry about connectivity in those places. I was married, but because of my over-involvement in work, I couldn't save it.'

Losses at work

Burnout stifles professional life just as it does personal life. Whether it is IG, Travis or Emily, their situations exemplify this reality. Over the course of time, they had become negative about their respective situations. IG had arrived at a point where he no longer cared about his boss's opinion. For anything he did, he was questioned and challenged to the point of inaction. Eventually, he took the position of not saying much in meetings. Gone was the spark that had lit up his performance. Same was the case with Travis, who had discovered that his seniors had vested interests. He started to disengage and lose motivation to take his business to new heights. Emily too noticed a decline in her performance and efficiency. Losing her boss's trust was a big setback for her.

All three of them exhibited what is called presentism: being physically present but not 'fully' there to engage in creative, forward-thinking reflection or good work. According to psychologist Barbara Fredrickson of the University of North Carolina at Chapel Hill, negative emotions—characteristic of burnout—can limit thought processing, diminish focus on new information, and impair the quality of decision-making.[6] All of which are counter-productive to an ideal performance and well-being.

And as this happens, it also impacts the functioning of others around burned-out people. Psychologically detached from work, they are less willing to help others and also less likely to receive help in return. Teamwork, collaboration and healthy discussions are no longer part of their repertoire.

Coming late to work, missing team meetings, not responding to messages, complaining about the organization or bad-mouthing the boss are some of the common traits among the burned-out group. Travis admitted to demonstrating these behaviours. 'I slowly built a wall around me. I didn't want to meet anyone for any discussion and I started to keep my office door shut. I was frustrated, cynical and extremely hurt with the behaviour of my superiors towards my work and performance. I felt that after years of good performance, I didn't get my due.'

On the other side of this continuum is absenteeism: when employees call in sick or when their physical and mental state prevents them from coming to work. A Canada Life Group Insurance study which aimed to understand the reasons for insurance claims being made by companies concluded that employee burnout caused by uneven work–life balance was one of the leading causes of absenteeism, and this had a direct impact on the bottom line.[7] In fact, a Centers for Disease Control and Prevention study shows such productivity losses cost employers $225.8 billion annually in the United States alone.[8]

Employee attrition or turnover is another price that organizations pay for burnout. There is loss of productivity, cost of recruiting a replacement, and time lost in bringing someone up to speed. Research by the Society for Human Resource Management indicates that every time a business replaces a salaried employee, it costs up to six to nine months' salary on average.[9] For a manager making $40,000 a year, that's $20,000 to $30,000 on recruiting and training expenses.

Watching leaders burn out and leave also significantly impacts employee and team morale. Sangeeta, one of IG's employees, was upset when she learned about his departure from the company. 'He was someone we all looked up to. We can't imagine the company without him. How will we achieve our objectives without his leadership? He was the engine who guided and took us along. We feel like abandoned children now.'

To prevent such impacts, some organizations spend substantial money and resources in creating supportive programmes for their employees. These initiatives range from coaching to providing people-friendly policies, to employee assistance programmes with an acute focus on personal health and well-being. Contrastingly, the failure of companies to take any action is indicative of inherent organizational flaws, where the leadership is seen as ineffective in creating a positive environment for employees. Because of which such organizations develop a reputation of being 'places not to work at'.

Societal costs

Needless to say, the cost of burnout affects systems everywhere: society-wide and countrywide.

Joel Goh, assistant professor of business administration at Harvard University, and his colleagues at Stanford University estimate that workplace stress is responsible for up to 8 per cent or $125–190 billion of national spending in the US on healthcare.[10] This includes the cost of tackling heart disease, stroke, asthma, high cholesterol, diabetes—the kind of ailments that contribute to 1,20,000 deaths a year in the country. The numbers look worse when we include the

$450–550 billion that, Gallup says, disengaged workers cost the country annually.[11]

You can only imagine the implications when employees are emotionally disconnected from their work; they are not performing and are instead negatively influencing co-workers, missing workdays, and driving customers away.

When it comes to physician burnout, this not only has a bearing on quality care, but also increases patient safety concerns and medical errors. This itself is estimated to cost $97–129 billion annually, according to a study led by Charles Andel, the manager of radiology quality and compliance at Loyola University Medical Center, Illinois.[12] Worse, you and I pay the unredeemable cost of lives lost because of such avoidable errors.

Besides this direct financial impact, there are intangible impacts too. Broken relationships, missed quality time with friends and family, loneliness and overall unhappiness are colossal societal concerns. Rising rates of divorces and single families because of burnout or other reasons have changed the experience of growing up for children. According to Judith Wallerstein, an American psychologist and the author of *The Unexpected Legacy of Divorce*, the relationship between husband and wife is essential for a healthy family relationship.[13] 'Children identify not only with their mother and father as separate individuals but with the relationship between them. They carry the template of this relationship into adulthood and use it to seek the image of their new family. Children in broken families feel less protected and less certain about their future as compared to those in reasonably good, intact families.'

Having said that, even in intact families, parent–child interactions aren't significantly high given the work–life challenges and pressures everyone is reeling under. A British study commissioned by Highland Spring—the UK's largest bottled water company—looked to understand the pressures that parents of today face. One of the findings was that parents and children spent an average of only thirty-four minutes a day as a family.[14]

What is ironical is that as leaders, we spend significantly more time coaching our employees, but so little coaching our own children who are to be the future leaders. A study by sociologists Melissa Milkie at the University of Toronto, Kei Nomaguchi from Bowling Green State University in Ohio, and Kathleen Denny of the University of Maryland showed that quality time between parents and children is associated with lower rates of delinquent behaviour, less drug and alcohol abuse, and higher academic grades.[15] They found that six hours a week of 'family time' made a significant difference to a teenager's well-being and achievements. Clearly an important takeaway for parents to consider.

Burnout also leads to a significant increase in loneliness. A 2018 study led by the global health service company Cigna that surveyed 20,000 US adults (aged eighteen and older) found that nearly 50 per cent of them suffered from feelings of loneliness.[16] The report described the impact of loneliness and social isolation as being 'twice as harmful as obesity, and comparable to smoking 15 cigarettes a day or being an alcoholic'.[17]

It is evident that burnout has become a systemic issue, impacting our lives at the personal, professional and social level. It strongly calls for action from each of us—individuals, organizations and societies at large—to facilitate a life of well-being that is characterized by robust energy, positive relationships and effective performance.

The big question is: how do we get there?

PART II

Individual Strategies to Beat Burnout

Be humane towards yourself

Attend to the stress or pain signals your
body is alerting you to

The four elements of the Well-being State
Pyramid are:

1) The Foundation
2) Physical Energy
3) Emotional Stability
4) Mental Focus

5

The Well-being State Pyramid: A Structured Approach to Get Started

W HAT MAKES SOMEONE sustain peak performance despite pressure and stress? What keeps them away from burnout and gives them a sense of well-being?

Management gurus and others have long sought to identify precisely what makes some people flourish and thrive, and others fail. Sure, there are environmental perks in the form of external rewards, recognition and growth opportunities, but we also know that they aren't necessarily the be-all and end-all for performance and well-being.

For one, there needs to be an inherent motivation and purpose to keep us going. Two—and this is often overlooked— optimal performance and well-being require enhanced levels of energy especially when we are working under pressure. So, unless we have our physical, emotional and mental faculties rowing in the same direction and with consistent velocity, we are unlikely to achieve our personal and professional goals. And when that happens, we get frustrated, stressed and burned out.

To avoid burnout, we have to intentionally and deliberately nurture a well-being state. A state that is laden with positive energies that allow us to function without costing us our relationships, health or other things that matter. According to Ed Diener, an American psychologist, well-being can be defined through three interrelated components: 'frequent positive affect, infrequent negative affect, and life satisfaction.'[1] Likewise, Huseyin Naci of the department of social policy, London School of Economics and Political Science, and John Loannidis of the department of medicine, Stanford Prevention Research Center, define it as: 'Physical, mental, and social health that includes choices and activities related to achieving physical vitality, mental clarity, social satisfaction, a sense of accomplishment, and personal fulfilment.'[2]

A common thread underlying these definitions is the positive evaluation of oneself across physical, mental, emotional and social domains. Well-being is everything that burnout isn't. It is about energy, accomplishments, high self-efficacy and connections, as opposed to exhaustion, cynicism, poor efficacy and isolation.

To beat burnout, I propose a framework called the Well-being State Pyramid (WSP). It embodies the principle of being humane towards yourself. Being kind and considerate towards *you*; taking care of your health, needs and demands; addressing the stresses or the many alerts the body or mind may be giving you; taking timely action and proactively strengthening your whole self to tackle day-to-day challenging situations.

There are two parts to this framework: the foundation and three levels.

Accountability, purpose and priorities make the foundation of the pyramid. To prevent burnout or to live a life of well-being, you need to hold yourself accountable. Unless you take the responsibility, no change will occur. Identifying your purpose and knowing your priorities make the other two components of the foundation. Together, they serve as a guiding post for all your choices and future actions.

Physical, emotional and mental energies represent the three levels of the pyramid. By actively enhancing each of them, you can effectively and efficiently live your purpose and manage your priorities, all without getting burned out. As you do this repeatedly, you enhance your well-being, characterized by health, satisfaction, a sense of accomplishment and personal fulfilment.

Well-being State Pyramid

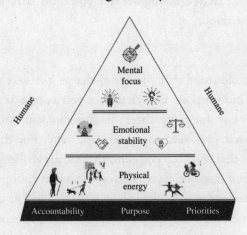

Humane

Let's take a detailed look at each of these elements.

Accountability

The most important aspect of living a burnout-free life is taking ownership. Only by taking personal responsibility can you enable a change. Research by psychologists Megan Oaten and Ken Cheng of Macquarie University, Sydney, shows that control and health are positively linked.[3] The more you control things for yourself or take accountability, the less stressed or worried you feel. Conversely, a belief that you can't do anything about your situation, or that someone else is responsible for your plight, only leads to more complaining, stress and burnout.

So the very first move towards a burnout-free life is to hold yourself accountable. If you are burned out, heading towards burnout, or are simply not content with how things are going for you, take charge. Recognize that you control the situation, no one else does.

Purpose

Having understood that you are in charge, the next step is to identify your purpose. One that gives you a sense of direction and the reason for going 'there'. In doing so, you would know exactly what you want to achieve and why. For that is the motivator that will keep you going despite the challenges along the way. For instance, if you are very clear that your purpose is to make tons of money, then all your actions will be driven by that purpose. You may choose to do overtime, take on stretch assignments, and not mind the overwork because you know you will be paid handsomely. On the other hand, if your intent is to positively impact others' lives, you won't worry about money but rather seek opportunities to live by your purpose. Your whole perspective shifts with your purpose.

In the absence of purpose, though, you don't know which direction to take. You do all sorts of things—put in extended hours and take on too much—all without discerning what you actually want, and hence may remain frustrated despite giving it your all. To beat burnout and achieve or regain control over well-being, identifying your purpose is vital.

Priorities

Knowing what things are important or matter to you is another critical aspect of this foundation. There are so many things you may want to do, but that simply isn't possible given the limited time and energy at your disposal. By putting your hands in everything, you will only end up compromising your effectiveness and the outcomes. It is in your best interest to focus on the critical few that truly make you happy or align with your purpose. Whether your priorities are towards your family, work, health, community or something else, calling them out and acknowledging them will keep you focused.

In sum, holding yourself accountable, knowing your purpose, and focusing on priorities that matter to you initiate the process of beating burnout. But to execute these, you also need your physical, emotional and mental capacities working in tandem, in your favour. As Dr Huseyin Naci, referenced above, noted, you need all three to achieve personal fulfilment. Deficiency in any or all those aspects would lead to dissatisfaction and burnout.

Physical energy

The bottom rung of the pyramid is about augmenting your physical energies so you have the fuel to go through the day with full vitality. When you feel energetic, you are better equipped to tackle situations and challenges.

To achieve a state of well-being, raise your energy levels by taking care of your physical needs through balanced meals, adequate sleep and regular exercise.

Emotional stability

With physical resources in place, the next rung of the pyramid is about strengthening your emotional capabilities. Regulated or balanced emotions help you respond mindfully, even under the toughest conditions. The more positive and stable you feel, the better you respond to situations.

Emotional stability can be built by thinking positive, practising mindfulness, engaging in acts of gratitude and giving, laughing, and leveraging relationships to share your highs and lows. Individually and collectively, they facilitate emotional regulation and serve as coping mechanisms to mitigate burnout.

Mental focus

The third and top rung of the pyramid relates to sharpening your mental focus. A state that allows you to rummage through clutter, think, reason, comprehend and deliver without becoming overwhelmed. It's all about working smartly: introducing efficiencies to free up time and preserving your energy resources. Leveraging to-do lists and calendars, staying out of your inbox, taking adequate breaks and time off, and managing technology appropriately, for example, can reduce stress and in the process prevent burnout.

Together, the three levels of the WSP work towards achieving a heightened sense of well-being. Though they appear distinct, they are interrelated. You need optimal physical and emotional resources to solve business problems. Likewise, you need emotional stability to recognize that your body requires rest or fuel to function effectively. Similarly, mental clarity will better facilitate your emotional and physical response to situations.

The best performers tap into positive energy at all levels of the pyramid.

Though the WSP addresses beating burnout from an individual's vantage, there is more that requires attention. The environment we are a part of—our organization and society as a whole—also needs to change. Humane work cultures, caring leaders, supportive work policies and countrywide regulations can aid in beating burnout.

The following chapters will illustrate science-backed individual and environmental strategies to beat burnout and regain control over our well-being.

The Foundation

Don't Be a Victim, Hold Yourself Accountable
Find Your Purpose
Know Your Priorities

You are accountable for your well-being

Exit the environment that's causing you grief
or find something to like about it

Enhance your accountability by defining
your goals, observing others, asking for
feedback, and keeping an upbeat mood

6

Don't Be a Victim, Hold Yourself Accountable

ARE YOU A victim or are you accountable?

Several years ago, this was a popular tagline in my company's strategy rollout. All our offices were strewn with 'accountable–victim' charts as on the following page.[1] The bottom of the ladder depicts a victim's mindset, and the top an accountable one. The intent was to hone a culture of accountability, to take ownership rather than blame others or be passive about our inefficiencies.

Needless to say, the company wanted us to be at the top end of the ladder rather than the bottom.

One of the examples used to drive home the importance of this message was personal safety. Sure, the organization could make the facilities as safe as possible, but ultimately we had to follow rules and practices to ensure our own safety. No one else was accountable for this or could do it for us. Not

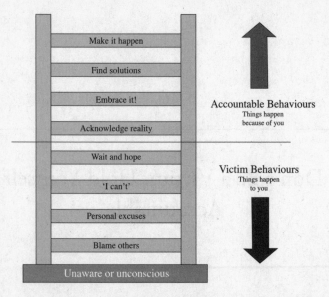

Source: https://www.forbes.com/sites/rodgerdeanduncan/2018/05/04/avoid-the-blame-game-be-accountable-for-accountability/#150221392b22

the boss, the company or anyone else. Downstream, this very mindset of owning our safety translated into zero accidents, high quality work and on-time product delivery.

The concept of an accountable–victim mindset was also beautifully illustrated by psychologist Martin Seligman and his colleagues through experiments conducted on dogs.[2] Decades ago, in one experiment, they placed a dog in a special cage that had a low barrier dividing the cage into two compartments. The floor of each half of the box had an electrical grid that could deliver a painful shock to the dog. The researchers could flip a switch to direct the electrical current to either Compartment A or Compartment B.

When the researchers turned on the electrical current in Compartment A, the dog jumped around frantically until it accidentally jumped over the barrier into Compartment B, escaping the shock. When they switched the current to Compartment B, once again the dog jumped around randomly until it accidentally crossed the barrier to safety. After a few trials, the dog learned to expect the shock and would cross the barrier more quickly after the current was turned on. This was called 'escape learning', because the dog was learning to escape from the shock.

In another experiment, Seligman strapped some of the dogs into a hammock and gave them inescapable shocks at random intervals. The next day, when these dogs were tested in that special box, their behaviour was very different from that of the previous set of dogs. These dogs would jump around frantically as soon as they felt the shock, but after a few seconds they would stop moving, lie down and begin to whine. They cowered as if without hope. Their conditioning was so powerful that they had formed the expectation that they could not control their environment. He called this behaviour 'learned helplessness'. The dogs behaved as victims of their situation.

As with the dogs, learned helplessness is very much a part of our repertoire as well. In 1986, a study was done with a sample of elderly nursing home residents to assess the relationship between exercising control and health.[3] Professor Judith Rodin from Yale University found that those who believed they didn't have control over their activities showed greater stress, worry and self-blame compared to those who exercised control. In fact, 93 per cent of those encouraged to exert more control became more alert, active and happy.

The positive connect between control and outcome is attributed to the fact that giving up or perceiving lack of control on the environment evokes an outpouring of stress hormones, raises blood pressure and lowers immune responses, thereby impacting overall health and performance.

Burnout too can be looked at through this lens. As a victim, you can blame the environment for your state. You can wallow in the belief that your boss, job, technology, society, etc. are responsible for your condition. Or you can take charge and acknowledge that only you are responsible for your condition, no one else is, despite the external challenges.

Recognize that:

- If you are swamped with work, you made the choice to accept it.
- If the work you do doesn't offer any excitement, it is a choice you made.
- If there are issues between you and your boss, you made a choice to stick around.
- If you don't like the organization you work for, again, it is a choice you made.
- If you are burned out, you made the choice to fall into it.

Because the decision to opt out or not rests with you; no one is forcibly keeping you there.

Geoff Turk, a senior leader in one of the organizations where I worked, observed, 'Burnout only happens to those who let it happen to them. Who ignore the pain they are going through. I know of many who are burned out, hate their jobs and yet they stick around. They believe their boss will change or work will shrink one fine day. These people are victims and refuse to take responsibility for resolving their issues. They only continue to sink deeper and deeper. Then there are others, who at the very first instance, recognize that this isn't the place they want to be. They engage in self-renewal, reframe their perspective, or exit, for they know what is more important to them and why. They hold themselves accountable.'

Recognizing that the primary solution rests in your hands and not in someone else's is a start in embracing an accountable mindset. As Geoff stated, this could mean two things: removing the environmental triggers that act as obstacles or removing yourself from that very situation.

Marshall Goldsmith, a renowned leadership coach, once told me, 'If you are in a situation where you are not happy, try to find something to like about it. Look at the positives; don't focus on the negatives. Maybe the work is good, or maybe the salary is, even though the boss isn't your type. This realization may free your mind from negativity and help you accept the present with peace. However, if the going gets tough, exit that situation. That call is in your hands. And once made, be happy about it.'

But we also know that taking responsibility is easier said than done. It requires courage and commitment to follow through. It is far easier to blame others and absolve yourself from taking any action. Take the case of a senior leader who has had an active career of over twenty years in a consumer product company in Bengaluru and took a break for three months. As he was a good friend of mine, I would periodically check on him.

This was how one of our interactions went:

Me (chirpily): How are you doing?

He: What do you expect? I'm just waiting for time to go by, fast.

Me: Enjoy the break!

He: It's so boring. I want to get back to work.

Me: Why don't you do something interesting to relax?

He: I didn't cultivate any hobbies.

Me: You can pick one now.

He: It's too late now.

Me: How about reading books?

He: I have already read many.

Me: Get new ones.

He: Who is going to go out and buy them?

Me: You can order online.

He: I don't like online shopping.

Me: Do you listen to music or podcasts?

He: I have a hearing problem.

Me: How about watching movies with subtitles?

He: I am not an invalid.

Me: Well, you are a writer. Why not pick that as an activity?

He: I am done with that part of life. No more of that.

Me: Why not call your friends over once in a while?

He: My wife doesn't like that.

Me: Why don't you go out and meet them?

He: I can't drive any more.

Me: Get a driver then.

He: Who is going to go through the trouble of finding one?

Me: Maybe go for walks in the evenings?

He: Have you seen what the weather's like? It's so hot. It will kill me.

And the conversation would continue with no clear solution to his boredom. He was part of the problem in refusing to take any responsibility for his situation.

Then there is Livette, a thirty-five-year-old sales executive in a local company in New Delhi who had internalized that life was unfair to her. I met her through a friend over a year and a half ago. That spring afternoon, she joined us for lunch and shared how busy and stressed she was compared to her colleagues.

'I leave work every night around 9 p.m. while my colleagues leave by 5 p.m. It is so unfair.'

'Who is stopping you from leaving early?' my friend asked.

'No one. I am working hard so I can get promoted,' she said.

'Then working late is not a sign of unfairness. It is a choice you made,' pointed out my logical friend.

'Yes, but it's still unfair,' Livette whined. She had donned the victim's hat.

Though the victim's hat may be pretty, it clearly doesn't serve the purpose of getting you out of adverse situations.

On the other side of the accountability spectrum is Dr Tony Avellino, who I have mentioned before. He said, 'I understood the importance of accountability after months of being in depression, and when I was minutes away from taking my life. I literally had to pick myself up and say,

"Enough, I am going to come out of this for the sake of my family." I sought help from my friends and counsellors, and diligently did everything I was advised to do. I transformed my lifestyle because it was a matter of survival. It was hard, but then I had only two choices: fight it or drown in it. I picked the former.'

Whether it is burnout or any other adversity, the protocol of accountability remains the same, says Ed Rapp, a former Caterpillar executive. 'When life throws a curveball at you, you have to find a way to manage the ripple effects it creates. Others can empathize with you but not resolve your issues. Only you can pick your life—no one else can or will.'

Having understood the importance of accountability in driving a change, how does one build accountability?

By believing in yourself and having the confidence in your ability to enable a change.

In the 1970s, psychologist Albert Bandura came up with a concept called self-efficacy.[4] He defined it as an individual's belief in his or her ability to successfully perform specific tasks. He posited that those with high efficacy are more likely to view difficult tasks as a challenge and put a high degree of effort in order to meet their commitments. They also recover quickly from setbacks and are more likely to achieve their personal goals as a result. They are accountable. Contrastingly, those with low self-efficacy believe they cannot be successful and thus are less likely to make a concerted effort (learned helplessness); they may regard challenging tasks as threats to be avoided.

The senior leader and Livette, mentioned earlier, exemplify poor self-efficacy: blaming 'external' factors for their unfortunate situations. Contrastingly, Tony and Ed demonstrate high self-efficacy or accountability in being open to change.

The good news, according to Bandura, is that self-efficacy can be developed. He proposed four steps to do so: mastery of experiences, learning from others, seeking feedback and staying in an upbeat mood. Given the connect between efficacy and accountability, the same steps are applicable to building accountability as well.

Master experiences

This is about building a repertoire of successful experiences, along the lines of 'success begets success'. Past wins or successful experiences can motivate and heighten your belief in yourself. For example, if you were successful in doing a specific task before, you can recall that experience and convince yourself saying, 'If I could do it then, I can do it now.' This reminder will give you the confidence to take a chance yet again.

Successful experiences can be built slowly, over time. Small wins will give you the confidence to pursue and persevere. As you collect small wins in abundance, you begin to believe in your ability to master larger challenges.

Here's an example. With all the typical time constraints as a mother of two demanding children under the age of five, Amy decided to integrate a meditation routine into her day. 'There was never a window of free time on my calendar. I started doing it for five minutes, just before my kids woke up in the morning. Those five minutes made such a big difference not only in terms of keeping me collected, but also heightening my confidence that I could do this every day. That motivated me to stretch my limits. I started getting up fifteen minutes earlier so I could extend my meditation duration. It has been over five months since I started this regimen. I have never felt better.'

When it comes to beating burnout, start out by winning with small changes.

Observe others

Observing others succeed in streamlining their lives can encourage you to take charge of yourself. For example, if your co-worker, despite his or her usual busyness, is able to make time for exercise, this may increase your confidence in believing: 'If she can do it, I can too.'

This learning is most effective when you observe someone who is similar to you. For example, watching Michael Jordan dunk a basketball might not increase your confidence in being able to dunk as well if you are only 5 feet 2 inches tall. But if you observe a basketball player with physical characteristics similar to yourself, that can be quite persuasive.

Find someone similar to you—in job profile, experience or age—who has been successful in changing their behaviour. Study how they succeed: the tactics and skills they leverage to perform well, how they continue to manage their time, focus on health or anything else that matters to you. Integrate those strategies into your interactions and routines. This is one place where you can copy and paste!

Ask for feedback

Family, friends and colleagues can also help boost your accountability. Notice how you feel when someone says, 'You can do it,' or 'You are so good at it.' These positive affirmations make you believe in yourself. They give you the confidence that you are capable of succeeding.

I distinctly recall a conversation with two of my colleagues when I was trying to define my purpose. They independently offered me insights about how they saw me, what I was good at, and where my strengths lay. They gave specific examples that affirmed my calibre in those areas. That feedback and evidence not only helped me set a direction for myself but also made me accountable to follow my purpose with full enthusiasm.

Keep upbeat moods

Positive moods can make you receptive and open to challenges; anxiety can totally undermine that. What happens when you are anxious? You are nervous, overcome with self-doubt, and just want to run away. Your confidence is at its lowest ebb, and with all the negative baggage and chatter, you get stressed and perform poorly. On the other hand, when you are upbeat and excited, you feel in charge, in control, and are ready to change the world.

Given the mind games you play with yourself, it is in your best interests to pump yourself up when you begin to doubt yourself. Engage in activities or surround yourself with people who can elevate your mood. And as you take on a challenge and deliver successfully on it, that will only add to your 'mastery list' or inventory of successful experiences.

Additionally, writing out your SMART goals can also enhance your accountability. The acronym stands for Specific, Measurable, Attainable, Realistic, Timely goals. By committing to and fulfilling your goals, you will create success experiences that will further enhance your efficacy and accountability.

Self-efficacy and accountability go hand in hand. When you believe in yourself, you hold yourself accountable. And when you hold yourself accountable, you heighten your self-efficacy. View burnout as a challenge; acknowledge it and find solutions to beat it. Hold yourself accountable to fighting it.

Find your purpose

It will give you a sense of direction
and meaning

Share your purpose with your family

7

Find Your Purpose

THE FIRST TIME I heard the word 'purpose' beyond a casual usage was over six years ago. Two consultants walked into my office to talk about floating a training on 'finding your purpose'. I admit I was sceptical at first; another corporate buzzword, I thought.

But, twenty minutes later, I was sold. I saw the link between purpose and performance, purpose and engagement, purpose and decision-making, purpose and well-being. It all fell into place. I could connect the concept with specific leaders in my organization who had succeeded in keeping their heads above water.

Empirical work also highlights this connection. The Energy Project, an engagement and performance firm in the US, surveyed more than 12,000 employees across a broad range of companies and industries to understand the link between purpose and work satisfaction.[1] It revealed that employees who derive meaning from their work are more than three times as likely to stay with their organizations. They also report 1.7 times higher job satisfaction and are 1.4 times more engaged at work.

Recently, I met Suresh, a business tycoon who confessed to being burned out. Referred to as a 'king of real estate' who had built an empire from scratch, he had had enough. At the age of fifty-five, he was overworked, physically exhausted and emotionally fatigued. 'I have come to realize I have been chasing the wrong things in life. I have made plenty of money, earned awards, but for what? I am divorced and have children with whom I don't share a good relationship. Nor do I have very many good friends to fall back on. Obviously, I didn't invest my energies in the right things.'

He continued, 'I have worked hard for over twenty years but deep down, that isn't gratifying for me. What is the use of money if I don't feel good making or spending it? I have lost all my enthusiasm for work. I keep thinking if this is what I have to do for the rest of my life, I'll soon die. I want to get out of all this. I feel the world is caving in on me. I have to figure out what I want to do with my life. I need a direction. I have to find my purpose so I can anchor myself and allow that to govern my decisions from here on.'

What it is

Knowing your purpose has become an elite expectation. Anywhere and everywhere you go, people are talking about 'finding or knowing your purpose'. Whether it is your company, school or even financial advisers, everyone wants to know what your 'purpose' is. But despite the concept being in vogue, we hesitate to answer this query. We believe it is a deep question that deserves a deeper answer. We think there is something mystical about it that requires an intellectual response. But the mere fact that it is such a common question suggests there is something very basic to it.

What is purpose then?

In general, purpose is defined as an 'intent', 'objective', 'your vision', 'your reason for being', or 'your reason for getting up in the morning'. Across these variances, it is inclusive of the 'what' and 'why' of your actions. In the world of business, according to Jack Welch, 'Purpose is about knowing where you are going, why you are going there, and what's in it for you to go there.'[2] Collectively, purpose articulates a focus, action and motivation to get you to a particular destination.

This is why businesses define their purpose. They boldly communicate it through their vision statement—one intent, one objective—to reach their goals. It becomes a single safe channel to propel thousands of employees towards a common path. So, the organization moves in the chosen direction as opposed to being pulled in multiple directions and in the process stalling progress.

Similar is the idea behind your personal purpose. It sets the direction and articulates the reason(s) why you want to go there. With that clarity, your choices, decisions, what you do and don't, all get in sync to achieve that purpose. You are willing to go the extra mile or make trade-offs to achieve your goals. Contrastingly, an unclear purpose makes you flounder and pulls you in different directions. The result is that your priorities get mixed up. You get stressed, there is no progress, satisfaction or fulfilment despite the time and effort you put in.

Data shows that engaging in purposeful or meaningful work reduces incidents of burnout. Dr Tait Shanafelt, chief wellness officer at Stanford University, and colleagues explored this in a study of 465 faculty physicians.[3] They found that those who spent at least 20 per cent or one day a week of their time on aspects of work that were most meaningful to them—such as spending time with patients—had a rate of burnout that was roughly half of those who spent less than 20 per cent effort in meaningful work. Doesn't it make you wonder what these physicians are doing if not seeing their patients?

One of the most effervescent women I've met is a paediatrician in the Chicago area. Originally from India, she has been in the US for close to twenty years. Having turned fifty this year, she is happily married and is a mother of two college students. One of the things about her that stood out for me was that despite being a full-time professional, she had an active social life along with being engaged in many hobbies and social work. If I had to define her in one sentence, it would be: she worked hard and played hard.

As I got to know her, I learned that she joined this profession because of her love for children. Nothing makes her happier than making kids' lives free of pain. 'I love what I do. I have only one purpose and that is to take care of my patients. It's an amazing privilege to watch babies grow in front of me. I am truly following my purpose and passion.'

On burnout, she observed, 'There is no room for it in my life as there is no conflict between what I want to do and what I do. I am content looking after my patients and that's all there is. Unlike many, I am not in for the money. But if making money is your end goal, then you have no choice but to keep insane hours and also be happy with it. It should keep you going then. Burnout only happens when there is a conflict between your purpose and the work you do.'

This opinion was echoed by Ed Rapp: 'All of us have seen the value of a clear purpose or vision at work. Why not replicate that process in your personal life? My wife and I penned ours down when we were starting our family. It was important for us as a family to have one common purpose that we could hold ourselves accountable to. That purpose continued to serve as a compass for our decisions and actions as individuals and as a family.

'Everything I do is connected with my purpose. My actions are governed by it. As a result, work has never felt like a burden; it has only energized and motivated me.'

Even after retirement, to honour and abide by his purpose, Ed continues to seek opportunities to make an impact. Diagnosed with ALS (amyotrophic lateral sclerosis) three years ago, he has been actively engaged in furthering the cause and finding a solution for the same.

His purpose remains constant and noticeably beyond himself. 'At Caterpillar, I think I positively impacted employees and now I believe I have the opportunity to make a difference in what is a tough disease,' he remarked.

While people's purposes are often quite generous and benevolent in nature, they don't necessarily have to be so. They can be materialistic too. The purpose for Ryan, a manager at an MNC in Singapore, was, 'Making money. Loads of it.' He was very clear about it. Supporting a family of six that included his spouse, children and parents, he wanted to give them a life of luxury, he said.

'I want to make enough so my family can live comfortably. I want to be able to afford higher education and offer diverse experiences to my children. Something I didn't have myself. With this as my end goal, I work extremely hard and aim for rewards and promotions. On the side, I do consulting to supplement my earnings. Personally, I am very happy with this arrangement. I work hard during the week and on weekends I am with my family. Because of the good money, I am able to ignore the many deficiencies in my job or work environment. As long as I am paid well, I feel good. Yes, if the money wasn't good, that would be frustrating. I would look out for another job then. Right now, I am in a happy space.'

Clearly, having a purpose sets the direction. It gives you a focus and drive to go after something that is of importance to you. Moreover, you do that without getting stressed and burned out.

But what if you don't have a purpose?

No purpose?

If it's any consolation, you are not alone. The Energy Project survey study mentioned earlier found that for 50 per cent of the people surveyed, their work lacked a degree of meaning and significance.[4] Surely something to investigate.

But not having a purpose doesn't mean the end of the world or that you are any less significant than others. All it means is that you haven't found that *something* you wish to pursue with all your might and passion.

The good thing about this ignorance is that this internal search can take you closer to identifying your purpose. Let me tell you about Anisha, who didn't start out with a clear purpose but ended up finding one. Her mother narrated the experience to me.

Anisha, a twenty-three-year-old medical student, lived in the breezy city of Bengaluru with her parents. Her mother was a physician and her father worked in one of the companies in the vicinity. Growing up, Anisha saw her grandfather suffer from various illnesses. He wanted her to become a good doctor and jokingly used to say that she could take care of him when she grew up. From that time on, Anisha wanted to become a doctor. With hard work, she got admission in one of Bengaluru's medical colleges.

Three years into studying medicine, in January 2015, Anisha took on a year-long internship. Along with this, she was preparing for her US entrance exams for admission to a residency programme. As she juggled everything, her concentration and sleep were affected. Ignoring those signs of exhaustion, she continued with her studies, wrote her first exam in September, and cleared it. However, post that, she couldn't motivate herself to prepare for the remainder of the exams, interviews, research, etc. to fulfil the admission requirements.

The stress of it all was impacting her. Anisha was losing weight, not sleeping well and was extremely anxious about her future. In October, she came to a grinding halt. She wanted to give up her studies.

'We were scared about her decision and also with what was happening to her. Anisha had never been like this before. This was not her usual temperament. She was always motivated and positive, and didn't allow stress to get to such extreme levels. Seeing her in this state, we supported her decision to take a break from studying and thoughtfully connected her with her mentors: her dance and music teachers who knew her since she was six years old. They were wise people who did what they did because of their passion, not for anything else. They focused on the process without worrying about the outcomes. We were confident that Anisha would connect with them about her issue,' her mother recounted.

The teachers worked on refining her dancing skills. Simultaneously, they guided her about life and the potential impact she could make in this world. After four months of daily training along with yoga and natural therapies, Anisha's interest and purpose in life began to rekindle. She started regaining confidence and believing in herself.

She acknowledged she was going to work hard towards becoming a good doctor. She was ready to tackle any challenges that came her way, she declared.

'We believe that dancing, which can be extremely cathartic and a clean break from study pressures, allowed her to think clearly. She came out strong and was prepared to take on any number of challenges,' said her relieved mother.

In April 2016, Anisha cleared all the admission requirements and enrolled herself in a residency programme in the US.

Every time she gets stressed or overwhelmed, she goes back to her purpose, reminding herself of why she chose this profession in the first place. That constant reminder and practising dance as a stress buster never fail to recharge and motivate her to keep going, shared her mother.

Unequivocally, a purpose sets the direction, and gives you the courage and motivation to continue the journey. Because of this clarity, you simply process the stressors and trade-offs differently, all the while keeping things in perspective. This is what Anisha did.

As a caveat, you don't have to experience an extreme situation like Anisha's to find your purpose. You can identify it in your current situation as well, as we will discuss below.

Get started

If you already have a purpose, that's great. Use this time to reflect on that. But if not, let's chart out how to go about it.

I'll admit that finding your purpose can be an overwhelming task. More so because the focus is on you. You have to reflect and in a way find yourself, who you are and what you want from life. This requires being brutally honest with yourself, which can be a daunting task. But, I promise, the effort is totally worth it.

To get started, allocate at least thirty minutes of uninterrupted quiet time. Follow these steps created by Dr Jyoti Chhabra, a health scientist based in Connecticut.

Step 1: Ask questions

1. Make a list of ten things you enjoy and don't enjoy doing. Discard the latter.
2. List three things people appreciate you for.
3. Check if there is an alignment between what you enjoy and what people appreciate.
4. Write down what you dreamt of doing when you grew up.
5. List out what you dream of doing today.
6. Write down five things you will miss not accomplishing in this life in your final moments.

Don't worry about the length of your document. Give free rein to your thoughts.

Step 2: Identify common themes
Having written down your responses, study them to identify common themes. What are the recurring words or patterns?

Step 3: Write your purpose statement
String the common themes or words into a statement. It can be one to three sentences long. Here are a few examples to prime you:

'To be a teacher. And to be known for inspiring my students to be more than they thought they could be.'

—Oprah Winfrey[5]

'To have fun in [my] journey through life and learn from [my] mistakes.'

—Richard Branson

'To positively impact the people and responsibilities experienced throughout life.'

—Ed Rapp

'To make a positive impact in the lives of my family, friends and others.'

—My purpose

Can you draft yours now?

Don't get stressed or carried away by a desire to put together a purpose that sounds or looks good. All you need to do is write one that is true to you. It should not only resonate with you but also excite and motivate you to get started on it.

Step 4: Make it visual

To internalize or ensure it stands the test of time, continue reviewing your purpose. For easy access, make it visual. Write it out on a piece of paper and stick it in places where you can see it: your study room, computer or the bathroom mirror. By making it accessible, not only do you internalize it faster, but also keep in mind why you took on a specific challenge.

What is fascinating is that even if you don't look at it intently every day, you still benefit from this visualization. A team of researchers from the UK—Anthony Blanchfield, James Hardy and Sameule Marcora—studied the impact of this subliminal or unconscious visual cue on the perception of effort.[6] They conducted two experiments. In Experiment 1, thirteen individuals were subliminally primed with happy or sad faces as they cycled to exhaustion. Results revealed that individuals cycled significantly longer when unconsciously primed with happy faces. Similarly, in Experiment 2, subliminal priming with action words facilitated a significantly longer time before exhaustion.

In short, visualization even when you don't completely focus on the content can positively impact outcomes. By keeping your purpose in your line of vision, you will internalize and act on it faster.

Step 5: Live a purpose-driven life
While reminding yourself about your purpose is great, the rubber meets the road only when you act on it or live it.

To achieve that, seek opportunities and make choices that align with your purpose. Weed out things that don't fit in. By doing so, you will have focused energy and time to work on things that truly matter to you.

Other ways

While the above process is an ideal way to start from a blank slate, there are of course other ways to find your purpose.

Perhaps your purpose lies in the job you are currently doing. There's an old story about a janitor that John F. Kennedy ran into at NASA in 1962.[7] When the president asked him what he was doing, the man said, 'I'm helping put a man on the moon.' He believed he had a meaningful role in achieving his organization's overarching goal. Adopting a mindset of focusing on how your work makes an impact is certainly a good way to think about your purpose.

Zeroing in on how your work helps those you love can also help uncover your purpose, suggests research. Consider a study of women working in a coupon-processing factory in Mexico. Jochen Menges, a professor at Germany's Otto Beisheim School of Management, found that those who described their work as dull were generally less productive than those who said it was rewarding.[8] Interestingly, though, this difference disappeared for those in the former group who saw their work as a way to support their families: putting food on the table, paying bills, etc. With that attitude, they were just as productive and energized as the coupon processors who didn't mind the task in the first place.

This perspective completely aligns with Ryan's purpose. Recall, his intent was to make tons of money for his family.

Alternatively, slow down on your 'taking' tendencies and dial up acts of giving, says Jennifer Aaker of the Stanford Graduate School of Business.[9] The more you give, the more meaning and joy you are likely to find in the work you do. Similarly, Adam Grant of the University of Pennsylvania's Wharton School showed that people who see their work as a form of giving consistently rank their jobs as more meaningful.[10]

A recent article published in the *Journal of Positive Psychology* by Daryl Van Tongeren and his colleagues examined the relationship between giving and meaning.[11] They asked over 400 participants to report on how frequently they engaged in different altruistic behaviours, such as volunteering, and how meaningful their lives felt. The team found that participants who were more altruistic reported a greater sense of purpose and meaning in their lives. The reason for this, the authors observed, was that engaging in altruistic acts fulfilled their need of being social or forging new relationships with others.

Another factor that might come into play is detailed in a 2010 study.[12] According to authors Netta Weinstein and Richard Ryan of the department of psychology at the University of Rochester, when we choose to engage in prosocial actions, it helps to meet our basic psychological needs for autonomy (feeling that we have freely chosen our actions), competence (feeling that we are good and capable), and relatedness (feeling close to others). These emotions enhance our efficacy and simultaneously lower our stress levels and hence the tendency to burn out.

Together, the two studies suggest that altruism may be especially important for strengthening relationships and connecting with others.

Perhaps your purpose is lurking somewhere in your current job?

Make it a shared purpose

While identifying your purpose is great, making it a shared purpose is a lot better. In fact, it is absolutely vital to do that.

It was a balmy afternoon in downtown Chicago. The place was buzzing with people and traffic. People were whooshing off somewhere, hurriedly crossing the roads, nudging through the crowd, or simply smoking on the sidewalks.

I too was rushing to my lunch appointment. I had a meeting with Joe, managing director for the last seven years at a renowned global research and strategy advisory firm. He specialized in coaching organizations and individuals on burnout prevention. Most of his clients were CXOs representing large MNCs. I wanted to garner his insights on the subject, including how he was helping his clients come out of their burned-out state.

As we waited for lunch to arrive at our table, he shared high-level details of what some of his clients were going through. He talked about the collateral damage caused to the company and the personal challenges his clients were facing because of burnout.

'More and more executives are burning out primarily because roles and responsibilities are becoming larger and unmanageable. There is pressure to perform, to outsmart the competition, and make more money for the company. Leaders are exhausted, sleep-deprived, and struggling to manage their work and personal lives. Unable to function well, they are frustrated and may take their stress out on their families. A majority of my clients are dealing with relationship issues with their spouses and children. It is getting worse by the day.'

Joe remarked that his executives were alone on their runways. They had no support from anyone—their families or friends.

This wasn't a revealing find by any stretch. When you fail to bring your families along on what you want to do, why it is important to you, and more importantly, how they can support you through it, that creates a void in the marriage. Jackson and Maslach and others have shown this through their empirical work.[13]

Sharing your purpose with those who matter, those who can be potential allies and are likely to be impacted by what you do—and how you do it too—is critical for your well-being and success. Going back to Joe's clients, only a few of them had included their families in their purpose. It was apparent that there was a significant communication gap between them and their families when the early intervention work commenced. However, through focused work and facilitated communication between family members, measured and significant improvement occurred with several of the client leaders and their families.

A Wall Street trader I met at a data analytics seminar in New York told me, 'I was so preoccupied with my own goals and ambitions that it never occurred to me to discuss them with my wife. I assumed she would understand. After all, I was working this hard for her sake and the family's. I continued to work like there was no tomorrow, without realizing she wasn't with me. I hurt our marriage. I lost everything because of that one mistake.'

At the other end is Prashant, an engineering director at an aeronautics company in the US, who swears by the importance of sharing his purpose and keeping a balance with his family. 'Years ago, my wife and I discussed what we wanted to do and achieve in life. Our purpose was to work as one team in that journey. From that day to today, we have been supporting each other through all our commitments. That support helped me reach the peak of my career without getting burned out.'

To align your purpose, initiate a conversation with your family members: your spouse and significant others in your immediate circle. Bring them up to speed on what your purpose is, and how you and they can fulfil it, together. Not only would that initiate a dialogue but also bring out any concerns or potential trade-offs to be made in the process. Caren Baruch-Feldman of the department of psychology, St John's University, New York, and colleagues studied how social support from family, supervisors and co-workers can influence work outcomes.[14] They found that family support and burnout were inversely related. The more familial support there was, the less likelihood of burnout among the participants.

Makes sense, doesn't it? Families serve as a protective barrier and make supportive platforms for talking, sharing and learning.

Now, what happens if your family doesn't agree or refuses to align with your purpose? The logical approach would be to go back to the drawing board. This is similar to what you would have done at work when a stakeholder disagreed with your proposal. Take their input, tweak your purpose to reflect a shift from 'I' to 'us', and make it more palatable for everyone concerned. The goal is to converge to a common agreement before marching away on your merry way.

By sharing your purpose, you not only make the ride more enjoyable, but also lower your chances of burnout while keeping your relationships intact.

Every action has an equal and opposite
reaction

To give time to something, you take away
time from something else

Identify and focus on a few critical priorities

You will avoid stress and frustration

8

Know Your Priorities

THIRTY-SEVEN-YEAR-OLD MIYA, a mother of two young children, is a highly respected manager at an MNC in the US. When I met her, she was clocking over twelve-hour workdays. Getting home late, she found it difficult to fully engage with her family in the evenings. Her children, who were ten and twelve years old, would complain about her continued absence. 'It's no fun to eat dinner on your own. Why can't you be home early?'

'Even though my husband and babysitters are there to attend to them, I feel guilty about failing in my parental duties. The more I think, the more stressed I get. I feel like I am running on a treadmill with no pause or stop button. I am afraid I may fall one day,' she lamented.

Miya's experience is not uncommon. Several men and women are so consumed with work that other things take a back seat. There is a continuous search to find an optimal balance. If we slow down at work, there is that fear of missing out on opportunities, falling behind or losing it all. And if we don't, there is that risk of letting down those we love.

Part of leading a burnout-free life is to manage your priorities in alignment with your purpose. But to do that, you need to know what those priorities look like in the first place. Though we all have an idea about what matters to us, many a time, because of several competing demands, we tend to lose sight of it.

To bring them to the fore or to identify them, let me share an exercise that I learned many years ago in a workshop facilitated by the Centre of Creative Leadership in Bengaluru.

To get started, take a sheet of paper and draw a large circle in the middle of it. Divide it into slices that reflect where you spend the majority of your time each day. It could be time with your family, at work, pursuing hobbies or doing something else. Once that is done, allocate the percentage of time you spend in each of those slices. The sum total should be 100 per cent.

When Miya drew her pie, it looked like this: 90 per cent at work, 5 per cent with the family, and another 5 per cent in community work. Considering her goal was to spend more time with her family, this pie was clearly out of balance for her. It wasn't surprising that she was overwhelmed and close to burning out. Her current actions were heavily skewed towards work.

Now keep in mind that this very pie could work well for someone whose priority is to focus on work alone. In fact, I know of corporate leaders who find extreme joy and satisfaction in their work. All their time is devoted to that alone; nothing else matters. Importantly, they never experience burnout either. Their families have come to terms with their passion and support them through that.

Priorities: The Reality

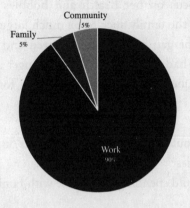

But Miya's situation was different. She wasn't happy with her situation. She was guilty and overwhelmed with her work and personal responsibilities.

Now, to depict what her desired life looked like, she drew another circle, this time depicting a life she wanted, an ideal life. Take a look at her pie now.

Priorities: Desired

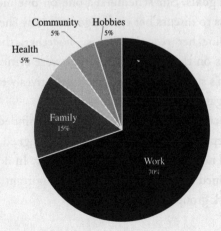

Her desired pie had more slices now. Besides family, she wanted to focus on her health and hobbies too. The pie also depicted the family slice to be much larger than before. Looking at the gap between her desired and current lives, she obviously had to make significant changes in her present. Some of the questions this exercise evoked for her were the following:

- Where would she find the time to focus on family, health and hobbies?
- What would spending more time with family look like to her?
- How would she manage her workload differently?
- Would she do more delegation or shave off some work from her portfolio?

Miya shared the following concrete actions she would take to get to her ideal life:

- **Revisit goals.** She scheduled a one-on-one meeting with her boss to discuss her challenges and how she wanted to streamline her responsibilities. Together, they decided to focus on the top five goals that were critical for their division's success. The rest of the initiatives were slated to be delegated to other resources.
- **Be selective.** To stay focused, Miya reminded herself of her purpose. She took on tasks that aligned with that, and did not raise her hand for everything. In doing so, she maintained her focus on what was important to her and her work group.

- **Set work boundaries.** Miya defined the hours she would be in the office. Earlier, she would leave the office when her work got done, after attending late-night meetings. Now, in the new design, she structured her work hours. Come in by 8 a.m. and leave by 5.30 p.m. Adding the commute time, she was home by 6.15 p.m.; that gave her enough time to focus on home and family. She got back to her computer after her kids went to bed.
- **Exercise twice a week.** She shortened her lunch break to accommodate exercise. She blocked her calendar for a thirty-minute period and hit the gym every Tuesday and Thursday. Her goal now is to increase this to three times a week.
- **Volunteer.** Miya continued volunteering at her children's school once a month, doing book reading sessions or helping fifth-graders with their science projects.
- **Unwind.** For her downtime, Miya took on gardening as a hobby. She grew a vegetable garden in her backyard. Physical work is a great stress buster, she observed.

Identifying and acting on these changes was a leap forward for Miya to get to her ideal life.

When we reconnected a couple of months later to find out how she was doing, she stated, 'It isn't easy to undo the years of habits, but I am slowly making changes one step at a time. Seeing this on paper has given me clarity on how skewed I was in terms of my priorities. I now feel light and in a much better position to control my hours and energy. I am definitely spending more time with my children and feel my work is more manageable than ever before.'

The beauty of designing your life exercise is that it gives you a real-time audit of what your life looks like now and the gap to get to your ideal life. It is also repeatable. You can adjust and alter your priorities with your changing circumstances. There are likely going to be moments when the work slice may get bigger and the others shrink. Or when health may take precedence over hobbies or something else. But at the end of it, you will be aware of the swings and know how to bring them back to equilibrium or to your preferred state.

What does your desired life look like? Do you have significant gaps to bridge?

Take a few minutes to write out the action items you will take to get to your desired life.

Reflection Points

1. Hold yourself accountable. No one but you can alter your situation.
2. Find your purpose. It will give you a sense of direction and reasons for persevering.
3. Distil your priorities. When you are clear about what's important to you, you will know exactly what to do and what not to.
4. Together, these actions will lower your stress and shield you from burnout.

Physical Energy

Eat Right for Good Performance
Get a Good Night's Sleep
Exercise

Food = Fuel

Healthy Food = Premium Fuel

The Good	The Bad
Three meals a day and a snack in between	Skipping meals
Whole grains, fibre, protein-enriched food	Junk and processed food
Lunch with colleagues and dinner with family	Eating in front of the computer or TV

9

Eat Right for Good Performance

'THANK YOU ALL for a great meeting. I appreciate your hard work.' Kanika ended her teleconference and hung up the phone.

Tiredly, she leaned back into the comfort of her chair. Today was the end of a two-month-long effort that she and others had put into the design of a strategic project. It had been gruelling, running pillar to post to gather data from accounting teams locally and globally to assess the market share for one of their product lines in Asia. With one milestone achieved, she could finally let her hair down for a few days at least, she thought.

Knowing that she had to get back to work, she got up to grab lunch from the cafeteria. Suddenly she realized it was 3 p.m. and that it would be closed. Dejectedly, she walked down to the vending machine and pulled out a pack of chips. This was becoming a habit of late—missing lunch, living on junk food, having a quick late dinner, and falling straight into bed. Her father, with whom she lived, was extremely upset with her, believing Kanika wasn't leading a healthy life. 'What is the use of working so hard when you can't even enjoy the fruits of your labour? You need energy to carry on. Where will it come from if you don't eat or sleep enough?' he would say.

In our hurry to meet deadlines and accomplish more, we don't pause to think how we are functioning or how we can even sustain that life. We are notorious for skipping meals, living on a few hours of sleep, and staying glued to our desks, laptops and phones. Not the right blend of fuel to keep us energized and healthy. And when we continue that way, it eventually takes a toll on our mental acuity, performance and well-being. Despite our smartness, we miss the obvious that body and mind are interrelated.

Without a doubt, food is the basic currency for survival. It regulates our energy levels, vitality and overall health. What we eat, when and how are critical to our functioning. Science suggests that eating fresh and nutritious food, avoiding fat-rich or sugar-laden items, and eating at regular intervals and mindfully are essential for a healthy body and mind. Experts in various committees of the American Heart Association assert that paying attention to how often we eat and at what time of the day we eat can help to lower risks of heart attack and stroke.[1]

But despite our access to this wisdom, we fail to integrate these suggestions into our daily lives. Blaming our hectic work schedules and life challenges, we simply don't take the time to enjoy and savour our meals. In a way, stress and healthy eating are inversely related. The more stressed we are, the less we focus on eating or eating right. A Finnish study led by Nina Nevanperä looked at the relationships between burnout, eating behaviour and weight in a sample of 230 working women.[2] They found that women experiencing burnout had significantly higher scores in emotional eating (eating due to external triggers) and uncontrolled eating (not being able to control the amount of food consumed) than those who were not burned out. The authors suggested that those experiencing burnout may be more vulnerable and have a hindered ability to make changes in their eating behaviour.

While emotional or binge eating is one part of the problem, not eating at all or skipping meals is another. According to a US study that surveyed 10,000 people, only 47 per cent ate breakfast daily, 40 per cent went straight to lunch and 39 per cent skipped dinner or lunch.[3] The main reasons given were 'Not hungry in the morning', or simply, 'Do not have time to eat.' Out of those who ate breakfast, convenience was the key. Almost half ate something on the go, 45 per cent got their breakfast from a fast food place, and 27 per cent opted for a coffee shop meal.

What happens when we skip meals because of our busyness? There is no energy or focus. The body's blood sugar decreases, which hinders our ability to think straight. The brain needs glucose to run efficiently and if there is not enough, the body does not function at its optimal best. We feel irritable, confused and tired. Simultaneously, the body begins to increase production of cortisol, leaving us stressed and angry.

One study led by Yunsheng Ma and team shows that skipping breakfast also means you may eat more later; it correlates to a higher daily caloric intake.[4] While calories don't necessarily mean obesity, researchers found that skipping breakfast was, in fact, associated with a higher risk of obesity. Those who skipped breakfast at least 75 per cent of their recorded days throughout the study were at 4.5 times higher risk of obesity. Further, skipping breakfast also means you get hungry before lunchtime. You reach out for a quick snack that is typically high in sugar and fat content—chips, chocolates, candy, muffins, etc.—thereby contributing to unhealthy weight gain and fake energy spikes.

Isn't it ironical that we put the best fuel in our cars but fail to do the same for our bodies? No surprise that our unhealthy eating habits can be at a significant cost to our health and well-being. Together, these ailments impact our moods, activity levels, interactions and productivity.

In an interesting study, Shai Danziger, Jonathan Levav and Liora Avnaim-Pessoa of the department of management, Ben Gurion University of the Negev, Israel, and Columbia Business School, Columbia University, New York, explored the link between meals and productivity.[5] They tested the common caricature of realism that justice is 'what the judge ate for breakfast'.

The team recorded the work routine of the study participants, who happened to be the judges. These judges took two daily food breaks, which segmented the deliberations of the day into three distinct 'decision sessions'. The findings revealed that judges gave harsher decisions when they were hungry or fared low on glucose levels. The percentage of favourable rulings dropped gradually from about 65 per cent to nearly zero and returned abruptly to 65 per cent after a meal break. The authors attributed this to effects of food intake, a short rest and positive moods. Imagine that!

Dr Lydia Chen, a general physician in her late thirties who worked at a Singapore hospital, shared how eating regularly made a difference in her productivity levels. 'Earlier on, because of lack of time and to satiate hunger pangs in the middle of the day, I used to buy candy bars from the nearest vending machine. Though they did the quick magic of spiking my energy levels, they brought them down equally quickly. Over time I put on weight and constantly felt lethargic, tired and unfocused. Being a doctor myself, I was aware of what was causing it all. To put a stop to this and be a good role model for my patients, I consciously forced myself to eat for better performance. The biggest modification I made was to eat all three meals and snack in between. Instead of depending on vending machines, I started bringing healthy snack of fruits and vegetables from home. This constant fuelling kept my energy levels constant. I was able to focus on work and felt less stressed.'

A balanced meal

Eating the right kind of food is as essential as the act of eating itself. Several studies highlight the extent to which food can affect our day-to-day experiences. High fibre, protein-filled and wholegrain-rich meals are associated with high alertness. Researchers Holt, Delargy, Lawton and Blundell from the University of Sydney, Australia, and the University of Leeds, UK, found that alertness spikes right after a high-fibre breakfast is consumed.[6] According to them, a good breakfast can be the difference between a lethargic, unproductive morning and an unstoppable, productive morning.

In another study, Andrew Smith from Cardiff University found that breakfast cereal consumption was associated with lower levels of depression, emotional distress and fatigue, as well as greater alertness, fewer cognitive problems and fewer bowel challenges.[7] These effects were noticeable after just one week of intervention.

Consuming non-rich foods also works in our favour. The digestive system doesn't use up all the energy to do its job then. If it used up all the energy digesting a heavy meal, not much would be left to focus on anything else. Eating the wrong food can take up to two hours or so to digest.

A team of researchers from New Zealand—Tamlin Conner, Kate Brookie, Aimee Richardson and Maria Polak—studied over 400 young adults who reported their food consumption, mood and behaviours over a period of thirteen days.[8] Afterwards, they looked at the way their food choices influenced their daily experiences. They found that the more fruits and vegetables people consumed (up to seven portions), the happier, more engaged and more creative they tended to be. Why? Fruits and vegetables contain vital nutrients that foster dopamine production, the neurotransmitter that plays a key role in the experience of bliss, motivation and positivity. The fibrous food provides antioxidants that minimize body inflammation, improve memory and enhance moods. Our mothers were right: veggies are integral to a healthy diet!

Caffeine, which many of us can't do without, also warrants moderation. Nearly two-thirds of Americans drink coffee every day, at an average of 2.7 cups per day per drinker, reports a Gallup study.[9] Though caffeine has a positive effect on our productivity—marked by higher energy levels, reduced fatigue and better alertness and focus in the short term—it also silently elevates the production of cortisol, the stress hormone, in our bodies. Too much caffeine can make us anxious and stress us out to make us see problems that don't exist, impair our sleep quality and impact our overall well-being.

According to Mayo Clinic experts, up to 400 milligrams of caffeine a day is safe for most healthy adults.[10] That roughly amounts to caffeine in four cups of brewed coffee or 10 cans of cola. Now, different people respond differently to caffeine. For some, even two cups can lead to jitteriness, distracting them from work and interfering with their sleep schedule. And for others, even six or eight may do nothing. So, depending on how one responds, the optimum intake can vary.

It is also recommended that caffeine not be taken at least eight to ten hours before going to bed, for it interferes with the sleep cycle. So if you typically sleep by 10 p.m., avoid caffeine after 2 p.m. To ward off stress or tiredness post this hour, simply walk around or talk to people. Both can naturally energize you.

In sum, to remain energetic and go through the day effectively, eat light and nutritious food. Walter Willet, the author of *Eat, Drink, and Be Healthy*, suggests the following to keep your energy levels full.

- Eat plenty of seasonal vegetables and fruits.
- Eat whole grains versus refined carbohydrates.
- Stay away from foods containing hydrogenated oils or junk food.
- Drink more water.

- Tea and coffee are okay, but sugar-sweetened soda and beverages aren't.
- Limit alcohol intake to moderate quantities.[11]

Besides the content of a meal, the quantity or portion matters too. Ancient wisdom suggests: eat breakfast like a king, lunch like a prince, and dinner like a pauper. There are scientific variations to this advice. Most recommend eating light, especially in the evening. Intersperse these three main meals with healthy snacks in between.

The art of eating

Now, eating or drinking is not just about pushing food down your throat. It is also about where you eat and the state of mind you eat in. Worrying and eating don't mix well. The brain creates chemicals that counteract effective digestion when we stress. Having a meal in the right state of mind—in a calm, happy and positive mood, and with a feeling of reverence and gratitude—is what makes a balanced meal wholesome.

Research encourages mindful eating, which is about paying attention to the taste, smell, colour and texture of your food. There are many benefits of this practice. A study by Gayle Timmerman and Adama Brown of the School of Nursing, University of Texas, Austin, showed that mindful eating promotes healthy eating habits that help control blood sugar and weight gain.[12] Similar results were reported by researchers Christian Jordan, Wan Wang, Linda Donatoni and Brian Meier from Wilfrid Laurier University, Ontario, and Gettysburg College, Pennsylvania.[13] Across four studies, they found a positive relation between mindfulness and healthier eating. It was associated with less impulsive eating, reduced calorie consumption and healthier snack choices for optimal energy levels.

Further, there are multiple benefits of having lunch away from your desk, with co-workers. Not only is social interaction healthy, it also allows you to stay plugged into what's happening within the organization. Not to forget, stepping away from your desk also allows you to stretch and get a much-needed break. According to Jennifer Newman, a workplace psychologist, eating together builds relationships that nurture support systems.[14] Workplace satisfaction is much higher if you eat with colleagues, suggests a study conducted by Brian Wansink, the director of Cornell University's Food and Brand Lab and his team.[15] They found significant positive correlations between work performance and eating together.

Eating with family is another best practice that has been touted by sociologists and family researchers. Correlational data shows that families that eat together are characterized by stronger marital bonds and better-adjusted children. In a sample of about 1300 youths, Jayne Fulkerson from the School of Nursing, University of Minnesota, and colleagues found that family connectedness, prioritization of family meals, and positive mealtime environments were significantly associated with the better psychological well-being of the family.[16] Eating together offers an avenue to keep the communication lines open. And if you didn't know this already, the positive effects of family dinner are undone by television viewing during meals, says a study led by Eileen FitzPatrick, of the Sage Colleges, Troy, New York state.[17]

So, consider family dinners an important ritual to eat right, divert your mind from work stress, and nurture communicative relationships with the family.

Based on these benefits, make time to eat for good performance.

Here are some guiding principles to get started.

- **Calendar your mealtimes.** Avoid accepting meetings during those times.
- **Eat breakfast.** Any time you think of rushing out of the door in the morning, stop and give yourself at least ten minutes to calmly sit down and eat. Start with a meal rich in protein and fibre, says Becky Ramsing of the Johns Hopkins Center for a Livable Future.[18] Eggs, nuts, dairy, lentils, oatmeal, wholegrain cereal are good choices.
- **Have lunch with colleagues.** Eat away from your desk and screens. Not only would that give you a break, but also allow you to interact and connect with others.
- **Decide what you will eat *before* you get hungry.** According to Dr Ron Friedman, psychologist and behavioural change expert, if you're going out to lunch, choose where you're eating in the morning, not at 12.30 p.m.[19] Because when you are very hungry, you will eat the first thing that you see. If you're cooking dinner, decide the menu beforehand. In fact, prep the stuff in the morning itself. We're a lot better at deciding to resist salt, calories

and fat if we have pre-decided it for a future time than in the present, says Dr Friedman.

- **Graze.** Don't wait for mealtimes. Spikes and drops in blood sugar are bad for energy and productivity. Smaller, more frequent meals maintain glucose at a more consistent level than a midday feast. Foods like oatmeal and most fruits and vegetables provide a steady release of glucose over hours. You can bring a bag of nuts or fruits from home and keep them in your line of vision for easy access to keep your blood glucose regulated throughout the day.

- **Have dinner with your family.** Make it a priority for your own well-being and to keep communication channels open among family members.

- **Go easy on caffeine.** It is good for productivity, but only when consumed in moderation. Consider skipping it as the day moves to a close.

The bottom line is, eat intelligently to beat burnout and enhance your well-being.

Sleep 7 to 9 hours to feel well and do well

IO

Get a Good Night's Sleep

'Life is a balance between rest and movement.'

—Osho

REST CAN TAKE several forms: sleep, naps or short breaks. Scientifically, the most robust form of rest is sleep. Commanding roughly one-third of our lives, it is a necessary requirement to run the other two-thirds of our life well. As we go through our chores, we burn calories, producing a lot of free radicals that are toxic to our neurons. It is during sleep that our body cleanses, consolidates, strengthens and stabilizes neural memory, and feeds creative thinking and performance.

But despite these many benefits, we skimp on sleep on the pretext of productivity.

I was only two weeks into my new job as a research analyst when I was asked by my manager to attend an all-employee meeting. The CEO was going to be sharing the breakthrough work the company was doing to bring new products to the market. An exciting topic for sure. I eagerly joined the crowd and found a seat in the fourth or fifth row of that packed room. About fifteen minutes into it, I found myself resisting waves of sleep. It was as if gravity was pulling my head down and beckoning me to close my eyes for just a few seconds. I wanted to so badly, but rationale defied it. I kept struggling and had no recollection of whether I did give in to the tyrant of sleep for those few seconds or not. The good news was that at some point I was free of the shackles of my body rhythm.

The next day, my boss called me to her office and told me, 'I heard from the marketing head that you were sleeping in the meeting.' Can you imagine my surprise and embarrassment! It looked like I did doze off and others had noticed, that too someone who had a say in my future. First impressions are hard to get rid of, I thought worriedly. Somehow, I waded through that conversation, apologizing for my behaviour. I was guilty of not having slept the past few nights for I was working towards a submission deadline for my thesis adviser.

Many of us have a tendency to compromise on sleep when we have work to do. Though sometimes these all-nighters work, in the long run they don't. We accumulate so much sleep debt that it becomes impossible to play catch-up or recover our health.

According to a poll conducted by the National Sleep Foundation,[1] 29 per cent of Americans fall asleep or feel sleepy at work, 36 per cent have nodded off while driving and 20 per cent have lost interest in sex because they are sleepy. Lack of sleep also comes with health consequences and challenges in completing work, both of which are known to augment stress levels. The reason for sleep deprivation has been attributed to prolonged work hours that often extend into late nights.

A team of researchers found that, on average, doctors in their sample got only 4.5 hours sleep during a thirty-two-hour shift[2]—a far cry from the seven to nine hours per night of sleep recommended by the American Academy of Sleep Medicine and the Sleep Research Society.[3] This makes the quality of care they provide to their patients a major concern. In fact, a 2007 Harvard report showed that preventable medical errors, which are primarily because of physicians and surgeons not getting enough sleep, cause more than a million injuries and between 50,000 and 1,00,000 deaths each year.[4]

In *The Sleep Revolution*, Arianna Huffington, co-founder of the Huffington Post, observed that we sacrifice sleep in the name of productivity, but ironically our loss of sleep, despite the extra hours we spend at work, adds up to eleven days of lost productivity or about $2280[5] per year per employee.

According to researchers at the research organization RAND Corporation, sleep deprivation lowers productivity levels and heightens the risk of mortality by 13 per cent.[6] The US loses an equivalent of around 1.2 million working days annually due to insufficient sleep. The study showed that nations can lose up to 3 per cent of their GDP due to insufficient sleep. If people started sleeping six to seven hours, this could add $226.4 billion to the US economy. Imagine what sleep could do for the global economy.

One 2010 study led by Mark Rosekind from Alertness Solutions, a consulting firm in California, observed over

4000 workers at four large American corporations.[7] As opposed to good sleepers, the ones with insufficient sleep experienced significant productivity losses, spending nearly three times as much of their day on time management alone. They were also less motivated, and had difficulty focusing, remembering things and making good decisions. Invariably, lack of sleep makes a perfect recipe for elevating stress levels and increasing the incidence of burnout.

What is the relationship between inadequate sleep and productivity?

Biologically, our bodies synchronize with a twenty-four-hour cycle of day and night by an internal clock called the circadian rhythm—from the Latin *circa* (about) and *diem* (day). As morning light approaches, light-sensitive retinal proteins get activated and they tell the brain to decrease the production of melatonin, a sleep-inducing hormone. Our body temperature rises, peaks during the day, dips in the early afternoon, and begins to drop again in the evening. Thinking and memory are at their best during the daily peak in circadian arousal. The reverse happens when we don't sleep. The body doesn't get a chance to rest or rebuild its reserves. Sooner or later, that exhaustion shows up in immediate episodes of decline in focus and productivity and, in the longer term, in multiple illnesses and burnout.

According to Mary Söderström and colleagues from the Karolinska Institutet, Stockholm, 'too little sleep (less than six hours)' constitutes the main risk factor for burnout.[8]

Plenty of research also points out the positive link between sleep and better health. A team of researchers from Norway and

Sweden—Mirjam Ekstedta, Marie Söderström and Torbjörn Åkerstedt—studied the role of sleep in burnout recovery. They looked at sixteen healthy controls and twenty-three white-collar workers who were on long-term sick leave (greater than three months) due to burnout. They were subjected to polysomnographic recordings—which capture brain waves, oxygen levels in the blood, heart rate and breathing, and eye and leg movements during sleep—at baseline and after six to twelve months' therapy. The findings showed that recovery from burnout was accompanied by improved sleep continuity and that the burnout group improved significantly on all the variables.[9]

Travis, the Singapore executive, validated this finding. 'Since I quit work after my burnout episode, I started sleeping without putting on the alarm. I would fall asleep at 10 p.m. and only wake up around noon the next day. This was very unlike me. Before, I used to average only five to six hours of sleep. Now, sleeping for over twelve hours is helping me recover. I feel more rested and calm.'

You are more focused and sharper at decision-making if rested, suggests a Washington State University study led by psychologist Paul Whitney.[10] In fact, the National Science Foundation shows that decision-making skills can improve by as much as 4 per cent with better sleep.[11] Likewise, research by Robert Stickgold, an associate professor at Harvard Medical School, and Jeffery Ellenbogen, chief of the sleep division at Massachusetts General Hospital, showed that people trained to perform tasks recall them better after a good night's sleep than after staying awake for several hours.[12] During slumber, our brain engages in data analysis, from strengthening memories to solving problems.

The same study also revealed that the consolidation of information that takes place only during sleep is 'essential for learning new information'. Being well rested protects against stress, reduces irritability and enhances feelings of well-being throughout the day. Not surprisingly then, in one Gallup survey, 63 per cent of the adults who reported getting the sleep they needed stated being very satisfied with their lives as compared to only 36 per cent of those who were sleep-deprived.[13] In a fascinating piece of research, psychologist and economist Daniel Kahneman and team from Princeton University found that less work pressure and a good night's sleep mattered more than money in their sample of working women.[14]

While a good night's sleep is critical, short naps can be just as effective in recharging us. Napping for just twenty to thirty minutes can improve creativity, focus and performance. In the 1990s, NASA recognized the crucial role of sleep for astronauts and experimented with short naps during their workdays. Led by David Dinges, a professor at the University of Pennsylvania School of Medicine, the study found that taking a twenty-six-minute nap while the co-pilot was in control boosted a pilot's alertness by 54 per cent.[15] According to NSF, today, the 'NASA nap' is a common practice among pilots making international flights for airlines such as Continental and British Airways. Likewise, companies such as Nike, Google and Zappos offer nap pods or quiet rooms for employees to rest and catch up on their sleep deficits.[16]

Shreya, an IT lead for a company in New Delhi who recently became a new mother, often catches up on sleep through short naps. 'I am awake in the night, so I try to make up for the loss during the day. I typically nap around lunchtime. A twenty-minute nap is refreshing enough to keep me going through the rest of the day and I am also better able to focus on my work as a result.'

For optimal performance and well-being:

- **Keep your sleep routines regular.** Be consistent with your sleeping and waking-up times.
- **Sleep for seven to nine hours.** This is recommended for healthy adults. Cutting down on sleep is akin to removing fuel from a car while intending to go faster. It is highly unproductive.
- **Engage in thirty minutes of moderate exercise.** This can even be brisk walking, says James Maas, a Cornell psychologist and the author of *Power Sleep*.[17] Exercise makes you sleep better.
- **Increase bright light exposure during the day.** Natural sunlight or bright light during the day helps keep your circadian rhythm or sleep–awake cycle healthy. This improves daytime energy as well as night-time sleep quality and duration.
- **Avoid caffeine late in the day.** Stop at 2 p.m. if going to bed at 10 p.m. As noted earlier, caffeine can block sleep-inducing chemicals in the brain and increase adrenaline production.

- **Avoid eating two hours before bed.** Eating activates blood sugar in the body, making us alert and awake—not an ideal state for a good night's rest.
- **Stay away from screens.** Keep smartphones and other gadgets out of the bedroom. A distraction, they also emit blue light that suppresses melatonin (sleep hormone) production. It makes the body believe that the sun is still up.
- **Prepare the ambience.** Keep the room cool. As night-time approaches, our body temperature naturally drops, indicating that it's time to slow down. By keeping your room cooler, you reinforce the body's natural instinct to fall asleep. If the room is too hot, it could block that signal and take longer for you to fall asleep. Most studies[18] agree that a temperature between 60 and 68 degrees Fahrenheit is optimal for sleeping, with temperatures above 75 degrees and below 54 degrees disruptive to sleep. Further, temperatures in the range of 60 to 68 degrees Fahrenheit stimulate the production of melatonin, which encourages sleep.
- **Unwind thirty minutes before sleeping.** Do things that relax you. Avoid responding to emails or reading/watching disturbing content. Instead, read a light book or listen to soothing music.
- **Practise mindfulness.** A study led by Dr David Black from the University of Southern California, Los Angeles, showed that a six-week mindfulness intervention with two hours a week led to better sleep.[19] In another study, Linda Carlson and Sheila Garland of the University of Calgary, Canada, found a positive link between an eight-

week mindfulness-based stress reduction programme and sleep quality among cancer patients. They also reported a significant reduction in stress, mood disturbance and fatigue.[20]

- **Catch up.** If you are getting to bed late in the night and forcing yourself to get up, just add fifteen minutes to your sleep each night to get back to a regular sleep pattern, says James Maas, the Cornell psychologist.

These practices underscore only one important point. If you rest well, you feel well and do well!

Exercise 5–7 times a week

Do what you enjoy doing

Make it a part of your job requirement

11

Exercise

Two realities are hitting us hard: overwork and sedentary lifestyles.

Unlike our ancestors, who were hunters and gatherers and always on the move, we are putting in long hours at work, and a majority of those sitting in front of our computers. Together, these two factors have significantly affected our activity patterns, eating habits, sleep cycles, stress levels and overall health, leading to obesity, diabetes, heart disease, muscular degeneration and several other ailments.

The link between work and health, while obvious, is not a linear one. There are several layers, as Yuichi Yamada, of the department of hygiene, Kanazawa Medical University, Japan, and colleagues, showed.[1] They highlighted three ways that work could specifically contribute to ill health: job stress may lead to unhealthy behaviours such as alcohol consumption or heavy smoking; sedentary work may lead to weight gain; stress may lead to modification of endocrinal factors related to weight gain; and long work hours or overtime may result in fatigue and weight gain.

As a snowball effect, these behaviours can impact our work and overall performance. In a Belgian workforce sample, researcher Michel Moreau and colleagues from the department of epidemiology and health promotion, School of Public Health, Brussels, found that those with high body fat are more prone to increased sick leave and long spells of absence from work.[2]

To explore the link between body mass index (BMI), healthcare costs and absenteeism, Wayne Burton and others from the departments of medicine and psychiatry, Northwestern University Medical School, and the University of Michigan Health Management Research Center undertook a study at a banking company.[3] They found that workers with high BMI had greater health risks—leading to short-term absences because of disability and illness—as well as higher healthcare costs than those who were not overweight.

In fact, Larry Tucker and Glenn Friedman from Brigham Young University, Utah, found that obese workers were 1.7 times more likely to experience a high level of absenteeism (defined as seven or more absences because of illness during the past six months).[4]

The implications of these findings are clear. When you work long hours, you don't exercise. With the result you are tired and lethargic, you gain weight, sub-optimize your immune system and are vulnerable to illnesses. As that happens, you are absent from work, which then impacts your performance and well-being.

Given these linkages, what can you do to break this cycle?

Science shows that to combat inactivity and other ailments, we need to get moving. Exercise for better health and better performance.

A study by Frank Penedo and Jason Dahn of the University of Miami, Florida, showed a positive link between physical activity and better quality of life and health outcomes.[5] Likewise, a Mayo Clinic report suggests that exercise is your answer to feeling good.[6] It raises immunity, improves mood, boosts energy, lowers stress, improves sex drive, promotes better sleep, facilitates social connects and is simply fun.

Beyond the physical benefits, there are cognitive benefits too. A Stanford University study by Candice Hogan, Jutta Mata and Laura Carstensen showed how physical activity is associated with improved affective experience and enhanced cognitive processing.[7] Moderate exercise in their sample was linked with increased levels of positive affect such as feeling alert and active. There was improved concentration, sharper memory, faster learning, mental stamina, enhanced creativity and lower stress among those who exercised. Further, a study by Lindsay Hoyt of the University of California, Berkeley, showed that high positive arousal or excitement because of exercise is linked to a steeper decline in cortisol levels throughout the day.[8]

If these findings aren't persuasive enough, also note that exercise can elevate your mood and make you feel less depressed. According to James Blumenthal and colleagues from, North Carolina University, Durham, exercise can be just as effective as the anti-depressant medication Zoloft in treating mild to moderate depression.[9] In their study, they found that though antidepressants may facilitate a more rapid initial recovery response than exercise, after sixteen weeks of treatment, the latter can be as effective in reducing depression.

Similarly, Frank Dimeo and colleagues at the Department of Sports Medicine, Berlin, found that those depressed patients in their sample who did thirty minutes of aerobic exercise daily had a 'substantial' mood improvement.[10] They attributed this to the fact that exercise lowers stress levels and facilitates the release of good hormones—endorphins and serotonin—that help the brain regulate moods.

These results make a strong business case for exercise, especially if your job requires teamwork and collaboration, and where feeling irritable or off is not an option.

Yoga

Beyond the typical exercises, yoga can do wonders to your well-being. The beauty of yoga is that it is more than a simple exercise. It is a full workout of the mind and body. You can do fast-paced yoga for a cardio effect, hot yoga for a sculpting effect, or restorative yoga for a relaxing impact.

Postures and breathing are fundamental to this form. They activate the parasympathetic nervous system that is the 'calming' or 'soothing' branch of our nervous system. Yoga is also known to improve muscle strength, flexibility, blood circulation and oxygen uptake. A perfect solution to gain fitness and strength.

Several researchers have looked into the benefits of yoga as an exercise and its link to well-being. Amber Li at

St Elizabeth's Medical Center, Massachusetts, and Carroll-Ann Goldsmith of the Harvard School of Public Health studied the role of yoga in mitigating stress and anxiety,[11] which showed a significant decrease in those following a yoga regimen.

On the other side of the waters, researchers A. Malathi and A. Damodran of the department of physiology at the Lokmanya Tilak Municipal Medical College and General Hospital, Mumbai, studied whether yoga could alleviate anxiety during routine activities and stressful situations, such as prior to an exam. They divided fifty first-year medical students into two groups: experimental and control. The former practised yoga for an hour thrice a week for three months. The control group was allowed to carry on with their work as usual. The authors found a significant reduction in the anxiety scores of the experimental group. The results pointed to the beneficial role of yoga not only in reducing basal anxiety levels but also lowering it under stressful situations, such as exam time.[12]

Even though research on yoga and performance isn't extensive and is marred with research design issues, there are studies as above that draw a positive link with well-being.

Fully knowing the benefits, what prevents us from exercising?

Barriers to exercise

For many of us, the answer is simple: we just don't have the time. Often, this is true and a legitimate explanation. There are weeks when work is overwhelming and deadlines are out of control, holding us back from exercising.

Take Nita, a lawyer in her mid-thirties at a private firm in Chicago. Between the demands of her job and her family, she had no time for herself. She shared her frustration: 'I am hustling the entire day from 5 a.m. to 9 p.m. Sure, you can say, why don't I exercise in the morning or the night? But I just don't have the motivation then. Every morning is like rushing to catch a train that is about to leave the station. I come back home tired after battling work and my commute. Somehow, I manage my family, but soon I am ready to collapse. I don't have the energy to exercise after a long, tiring day.'

In all fairness, this is typical life for the majority of us. But saying that we don't have the time only indicates that we don't consider exercise a priority. And this is where the problem lies. By not making it a priority or part of our job requirement, we treat it as a matter of choice: 'If I have the time' or 'After I finish my work.' What we don't realize is that if we exercise, we would not only feel more energetic and alive, but also be more productive at home and work; exercise counteracts stress.

So, instead of viewing exercise as a burden that takes you away from work or keeping it second to work, make it a part of work itself.

How do you successfully incorporate exercise into your routine? Here are a few research-based suggestions.

- **Make it a part of your job requirement.** Give exercise the same priority as you do your other business commitments. Integrate your exercise routine into your workday, in your calendar. That visibility will serve as a reminder for you to put on your gym shoes and get going.

- **Identify an activity you enjoy doing.** There are many ways to get moving other than hitting the gym or running on a treadmill. While you can eventually strive for a regimented, recommended thirty-minute exercise, for now, start with small and quick wins. Find a physical activity you enjoy and look forward to doing. Maybe it is going to the gym, running or playing a sport: tennis, basketball, cricket, etc. Or it may be swimming, dancing or yoga. When you genuinely enjoy doing an activity, the chances are you will stick to it. Conversely, if you feel it's a pain or constantly look at the clock for it to end, you are less likely to sustain it.

- **Schedule your workout for the morning.** When you exercise in the morning, you not only get it out of the way but also increase your energy for the rest of the day. In fact, a morning workout is a lot like eating breakfast in that it gets your metabolism going. It has been shown that people who work out in the morning are overall more likely to be consistent with their workouts. The reason being, if you wait to exercise in the evening you run the risk of being late from work, get overloaded with home chores, or simply feel too tired by the end of a long day. It's best to get it out of the way in the morning itself.

- **Work out at work.** Now, if you simply cannot exercise in the morning, commit to doing so in the afternoon or post work. There are different benefits of exercising during these hours.

    A quick run to the gym will energize and give you the bounce to get through the rest of the day. A UK study found that exercise during regular work hours may boost performance.[13] The researchers had over 200 employees in a variety of companies self-report their performance on a daily basis. They then looked at the differences within individual employees, comparing their output on days when they exercised to days when they didn't. They found that on the days when employees visited the gym, their experience at work changed. They reported managing their time more effectively, being more productive, having better interactions, and being more tolerant of stress.

Given these outcomes, pick a time that may be relatively slow for you: during lunch or before leaving for home. Calendar it and then stick to it.

- **Go for a walk.** If nothing else, go for a walk. According to psychologist Robert Thayer, even a ten-minute walk can stimulate two hours of increased well-being by raising energy levels and lowering tension.[14]

  Several colleagues of mine have taken up walking as a serious activity. They do everything to meet their target of 10,000–12,000 steps a day. They walk during the lunch hour, do walking meetings, walk to a colleague's desk rather than talk to them over the phone, take the stairs, or park their cars away from the office premises. In short, they go all out to find opportunities to walk.

  Now, if you take a walk outdoors, that's a bonus. Besides absorbing Vitamin D and enjoying nature, there are several emotional benefits too. Matthew Ballew and Allen Omoto from Claremont Graduate University, Claremont, California, found that a brief experience in nature can promote positive emotions, such as happiness, joy and feelings of awe.[15] All of which are known to reduce stress and calm the mind.

- **Create rituals.** To integrate exercise in your daily routine, create a personal ritual to help you. If you plan to exercise in the morning, break that preparation into small steps in chronological order. Here's an example:

  o Wake up at 5 a.m. or before your family wakes up to minimize distractions.
  o Change into your exercise gear.
  o Grab your water bottle and go to the gym or for a run.
  o Put on your favourite music or podcast, or simply focus on yourself or nature.
  o Set a programme on your exercise machine. If it's a run, have your path charted out beforehand.
  o Consistently, rotate through the same process or equipment daily. For example, the order may be running on the treadmill, biking, lifting weights, cool down, etc.
  o Shower and get ready for work.

  As you repeat these steps daily, they will become a habit. We will talk more about rituals in the 'Change Management' chapter.

- **Find a buddy.** Having someone motivate or encourage you can boost your interest in exercise, especially if you are unable to do it on your own. One of my colleagues formed a support group at his workplace. Four of them go to the gym together every afternoon at work. 'This teamwork helps. It's like giving a hand to pull each other up. We schedule this as a commitment and hold each other accountable for exercising and making progress. At the end of the month we review our exercise log and if someone is absent more than two times, he or she has to buy us all a drink. It is fun,' he asserted.

Having a personal trainer can have a similar impact. When you have paid money and know someone is waiting for you, you muster all your resources to get there on time. It's also a lot harder to back out on a friend or a trainer than to persuade yourself that just one day off couldn't hurt. You simply become more accountable.

- **Use other opportunities.** When you can, move. Instead of talking to your colleague on the phone, get up and go to their cubicle. Conduct standing meetings. Walk and talk. Trite as it may sound, park your car further away. Another one: take the stairs versus the elevator. When sitting at your desk, do a stretch. Do the 'one-arm hug', 'the knee jerk', 'touch your toes', 'the elbow pump', 'the backward clap', etc. Every movement counts. Remember, we were designed to be on the move, not sit at our desks for long hours.

- **Monitor.** Leverage the Fitbit and other devices or apps to monitor your steps, heart rate, etc. This builds accountability. Establish your baseline and slowly work upwards. In fact, you could make it a challenge for the entire family to meet a set target. Not only can that be fun, it can also encourage you to do more. Alternatively, in the absence of these gadgets, log your workout details— dates, duration, type of exercise, etc.—on a calendar. Write them out. This visual at the end of the month will show how regular you were. The idea is to motivate you further.

Now let's go back to Nita and find out what she did.

With full thought and deliberation, she made exercise a part of her job requirement. 'This was a mindset shift. I had never looked at exercise in this manner before,' she remarked. After weighing different options, she picked walking as her physical activity. She felt that wouldn't require a big change and she could comfortably utilize her lunch hour for it.

She started out by blocking twenty minutes on her calendar twice a week. 'This wasn't too hard to implement. All I had to do was change my shoes and walk out. I was hesitant at first, but then got comfortable with the fact that my team could always reach me over the phone. I started to enjoy the quiet time the walk offered. In Week 2, I added another day to my calendar. Depending on my work, I flexed the timing. Sometimes it was during lunch or at 4 p.m., which was a relatively slow time for me. After Week 4, I increased it to a daily walk. I have never felt this refreshed or recharged. I find myself humming on my way home, which is something new for me!'

Exercise is not optional. Just like you show up to work every day, show up to exercise. You will feel less fatigued and more energized.

Reflection Points

1. As the first level of the Well-being State Pyramid, physical energy is vital to carry out your daily functions. Lack of it can make you irritable, lethargic, stressed and less productive.

2. Just like a car, the body requires a constant input of quality fuel. Have three balanced meals a day and snack in between for full energy and vigour.
3. Again, just as a car overheats and needs time to cool down, your body needs the same. Rest and sleep are a must for effective functioning. Experts recommend seven to nine hours of sleep daily for it to repair and recharge.
4. Make exercise a part of your job requirement.
5. Start small and build it up to five to seven times a week.

Emotional Stability

Think Positive
Practise Mindfulness
Double up on Friends
Be Grateful and Give Back
Smile and Laugh

What you think is what you become

Reframe situations

Practise STOP

Visualize positive outcomes

Alter your posture to alter your thoughts

12

Think Positive

Watch your thoughts; they become words.
Watch your words; they become actions.
Watch your actions; they become habits.
Watch your habits; they become character.
Watch your character; it becomes your destiny.

—Lao Tzu

THE SEED OF burnout resides in our thoughts and emotions. How we perceive a situation and what value we attach to that determine whether we get stressed or not. If we read a situation as difficult, negative, ominous or out of our control, we are likely to get stressed and feel anxious, insecure and fearful. On the other hand, if we perceive it as a challenge, positive or exciting, we are more likely to enjoy the ride without experiencing any of the negative side effects.

Given the nature of work and the kind of busy lives we lead, we need to deploy a host of resources and effort to function effectively. And as we go through those experiences, they only make us stronger to fight spells of stress and burnouts. When we are emotionally stable or balanced, we hold positive thoughts, are optimistic and feel secure. Those personal resources protect and shield us, making us more resilient, strong and less prone to burnout. They in turn give us the confidence or the belief that we can take those challenges in our stride. Poor self-efficacy, in contrast, fills us with anxiety and stress. When we believe we cannot manage the daily hassles or serious issues, we fail to adapt to situations, do not respond flexibly, and react to situations without thought or enthusiasm.

Let me illustrate this with an example shared by a colleague of mine.

Sunita was giving an update on her strategy to a set of senior leaders in her office in Mumbai. A manager responsible for after-sales of one of the company's products, she had a team of three people supporting her. Midway through the slides, one of the six stakeholders, who was her boss's boss, spoke up, 'This isn't good enough. I am not convinced you can achieve your targets through this approach. We need to go back to the drawing board and restart.' He turned towards her boss and said sternly, 'Why didn't you prepare better? This was a waste of my time.' Without another word or explanation for what he wanted Sunita to rework, he moved on to the next presenter.

Based on the range of human emotions, Sunita had two ways to respond: get all upset, angry and disillusioned, or accept it gracefully. Given that she was in a room with senior leaders, she opted for the latter and continued being focused through the rest of the presentations. Once the meeting adjourned, her boss sought her out and said, 'How are you? Sorry about that outburst.' Sunita responded, 'I am fine. I am sure he is seeing something that I am not. I will set up a meeting with him and understand his concerns.' Smiling, she said, 'I will figure this out.'

What do you think? Would you have responded in this manner? I know of some who would have burst into tears.

Here are a few takeaways from this interaction:

- Sunita displayed calmness and balance.
- She didn't get upset.
- She adapted.
- She took the feedback in her stride.
- She didn't lose her confidence, remained secure in herself, and planned the next steps.
- She went ahead and scheduled a meeting with the big boss.

Does she seem like someone who could burn out? Not likely, based on this episode.

Now if it was someone who got all riled up, teary-eyed and frustrated, chances are he or she would be the type to get stressed with recurring challenging situations. All this would likely impact their moods, interactions and overall well-being and performance. They would carry this stress home, which would impact their family interactions, which in turn would stress them and impact their work further. This would create a vicious cycle, coming out of which would require significant effort and intervention.

Our response to situations is governed by our personalities or how we perceive the situation. Some of us just can't handle the minutest of stressors and some can face a tsunami of those. Some are simply positive in their outlook, and some are flooded with pessimism, which can completely drain their resources and impair performance.

But the good news is that with conscious effort, we can change how we respond to situations.

Inner thoughts

Our mind literally creates our world. You will agree that everything that happens in life is essentially neutral. It's a series of events that unfold without much inherent meaning, apart from what you ascribe to it. It is your assessment and interpretation of what happens that determines the way you experience it.

An Indian philosopher, B.K. Shivani, said, 'What we think is what we become.'[1] It is as though our cells are eavesdropping on our thoughts to become a self-fulfilling prophecy. Negative or belittling thoughts create an inner chatter that pulls you down; they heighten stress, and lower resilience and adaptation. There is research that validates this. Jessica Andrews-Hanna and others from the University of Colorado, Boulder, found that those who labelled their thoughts as more negative and more personally significant showed more negative emotions.[2] By contrast, those who saw them as more positive and less personally significant, improved their well-being.

Barbara Fredrickson, a social psychologist from the University of North Carolina in Chapel Hill who does research on emotions, showed that positive thoughts produce emotions such as joy, amusement, happiness, calm, gratitude and inspiration. They serve as nutrients for well-being that expand our awareness and ability to take in more of our surroundings. Negative emotions, on the other hand, narrow our perspectives. They constrict and obscure us from looking at the big picture, thereby impacting our mental states.[3]

Avoiding or beating burnout requires us to be in the flow of positive thoughts and emotions. This certainly does not mean you have to pretend or wear a mask but, rather, consciously appraise the situation while keeping things in perspective.

By accepting what is, and what can and cannot be changed, thoughts can keep us focused on the brighter side of things. A team of Portuguese researchers, Juliane Strack, Paulo Lopes, Francisco Esteves and Pablo Fernandez-Berrocal, found that professionals who were skilled at shifting their anxiety towards positivity were less likely to be frustrated or drained by their work compared to those who remained negative.[4] Those who were clear about their feelings were more likely to thrive on stress and possibly use them to achieve their goals and find satisfaction at work.

Sunita, the manager referenced above, clearly belonged to this group.

In another study, this same team of researchers also found that individuals who viewed their stress as excitement reported less emotional exhaustion, did better in exams and earned higher grades.

What does this indicate?

The trigger for stress and eventually burnout rests in our interpretation of the situation. One that we can control, should we want to. In the study above, how the individuals 'viewed' the situation didn't come from the outside; it stemmed very much from inside, from them. It was their desire to see it that way. While this can come naturally to some, others may have to put in some effort.

Our working models can be changed to what we want them to look like. The brain is highly malleable and capable of believing what we feed it.

Reframing

One of the strategies to change your perspective or thoughts is called reframing. Though the field of psychology is very detailed about it, put simply, reframing is a way of viewing and experiencing situations, ideas or emotions through positive alternatives. This can be done by finding something positive about a situation or infusing some humour into it.

Two Stanford psychologists, Andrea Samson and James Gross, conducted a study to explore whether positive or good-natured humour can be effective in taking the edge out of negative situations.[5] They showed the participants a series of unpleasant pictures twice. In Experiment 1, the participants simply viewed the pictures and rated their levels of positive and negative emotions. In Experiment 2, they were invited to view the pictures, and create a positive joke as well as a negative joke about them. What the researchers found was that the positive joke elicited positive emotions. The authors concluded that positive humour can aid in reframing whereby individuals shift their perspective of unfavourable events or circumstances to the positive side.

One of the strategies for reframing I picked up came from Angie Chew, the founder of Brahm Center in Singapore. Over a year ago, I attended a class on mindfulness facilitated by her. A petite Singaporean, Angie shared with us what she called the STOP mantra. She advised us to practise this whenever our thoughts gravitated towards negativity. This acronym translates into:

S: Stop for a moment.
T: Take a deep breath.
O: Look for options to reframe the negative.
P: Proceed with a more positive option.

To illustrate this, let's use Sunita's experience in that meeting room. When she heard the criticism from the big boss, perhaps she did the following:

- Stopped for a moment (to absorb what had just happened).
- Took a deep breath (to calm her nerves).
- Looked for options to reframe the situation (perhaps the boss knew something that she didn't; she gave him the benefit of the doubt).
- Proceeded with a positive thought ('I will figure it out').

I don't believe she found any humour in that situation, so let's stay away from that strategy for now!

Geoff Turk, the senior leader I have mentioned before, believes in the practice of reframing. He shared that if the situation is not under your control, how you look at it or respond to it can change how you feel about it. By recognizing that there is more to life than getting stressed about work and getting personal about it, you can divert your thoughts towards what indeed is good in that situation or in your life. He observed, 'When you go through personal adversities, you realize how small your promotions and work deadlines actually are. They are meaningless. To stay burned out even for a day is a complete disservice to what life has to offer to you. By deliberately reframing your perspective, you can beat burnout. You will begin to process the daily annoyances differently; you won't hold on to them.'

Visualization

Another approach to nudge our thoughts towards positivity is visualization: imagining positive outcomes. UK-based researcher Claire Eagleson and her colleagues tested the impact of visualization on those suffering from an anxiety disorder.[6] They asked one group to visualize an image of a positive outcome for each of the three worries they'd had in the past week, another group to think of verbal positive outcomes, and the last group to visualize any positive image whenever they started to worry.

Here's what they found. The two groups that visualized a positive image, whether it related to a specific worry or not, reported greater happiness and, restfulness and decreased anxiety. The authors concluded that visualization can literally reprogramme the neural circuitry of the brain and directly improve our emotions and the outcomes.

To beat burnout, visualize challenging situations with positive outcomes.

Power posing

Here's a test for you. You are sitting in a garden enjoying some sunshine. There are many people around, but you notice these two:

Person A is walking with short, shuffling steps, slouched shoulders, keeping his eyes downcast.

Person B is walking with long strides, arms swinging, shoulders squared, eyes looking straight ahead.

Who do you think is feeling good about life? As a hint, researcher Amy Cuddy from Harvard tells us that our posture speaks volumes about our state of mind.

You guessed it, the answer is Person B. He appears to be more positive, confident and willing to take life as it comes. In contrast, Person A looks closed-up and weighed down by burdens.

Amy Cuddy's research is fascinating. She recommends engaging in power poses—those that expand our body and give us a sense of power and control—to lift thoughts and moods. Simply by training yourself to sit, stand or walk a certain way, you can alter your thoughts and feelings. So how does this happen?

In one experiment, she and her colleagues tested whether changing posture before a high-stakes evaluation (for example, a job interview) can improve performance. Participants were asked to adopt expansive, open (high-power) poses, or closed (low-power) poses. They then prepared and delivered a speech to two evaluators as part of a mock job interview. Can you guess what they found?

High-power posers performed better. They exuded confidence and improved their chances of getting hired.[7]

Pablo Brinol, a psychologist at the University of Madrid, and colleagues at Ohio State University found similar results.[8] In their study, they asked seventy-one college students to either 'sit up straight' and 'push out their chest' or 'sit slouched forward' with their 'face looking at their knees'. While holding their assigned posture, they asked them to list either three positive or negative personal qualities they thought would contribute to their future job satisfaction and professional performance. Later, they were also asked to take a survey where they rated themselves on how well they thought they would perform as future professionals.

The study found that how the students rated themselves depended on the posture they adopted when they wrote their positive or negative traits. When students assumed the upright and confident position, they trusted their own thoughts irrespective of whether they were positive or negative. On the other hand, when they sat in a powerless position, they didn't trust anything they wrote down. According to the researchers, posture determines your confidence and belief levels.

What's the connect between external postures and internal confidence, you may ask?

Our postures alter our physiological make-up. They send a signal to the brain that impacts our hormone levels. In her study, Amy Cuddy found that among the high-power posers, there was an 8 per cent increase in testosterone and a 25 per cent decrease in cortisol. Together, that increased the feeling of power and tolerance for risk. The low-power posers, in contrast, showed a 10 per cent decrease in testosterone and a 15 per cent increase in cortisol levels.[9] They were clearly more stressed, which impacted their performance in the mock job interview.

Given this evidence, use your postures to your advantage. They alter your physiology and brain response. You slouch and think you suck, you will. You droop your shoulders and feel the stress, you will. You straighten them, you shrug off the weight and believe you can face the world head-on. Good posture makes for a happier brain. And a happier brain delivers positive outcomes.

Anytime you face a challenging situation—stressful meetings, difficult business problems or personal conflicts—engage in power posing: expansive, open, straight and balanced. Yoga can also help you practise open postures and get you in the flow of holding them at all times.

Leverage the quick strategies of reframing, STOP, visualization and power posing. They are easy and cost nothing to implement.

Mindfulness is about being 'present' or being 'in the moment'

It prevents us from ruminating about the past or worrying about the future

Start with 2 minutes of this practice daily

13

Practise Mindfulness

WHILE WE ARE on the subject of thoughts, it is pertinent to discuss mindfulness. We cannot ignore its power in keeping us centred and grounded. It is another way to tame thoughts and emotions.

I was in middle school, aeons ago, when I was first introduced to mindfulness. Engaging in this practice for ten minutes was mandatory in my school in New Delhi. Immediately after the school prayer, we were instructed to sit down, close our eyes, and pay attention to our thoughts and breathing. You can guess how effective we would have been at this. None of us liked this practice, which felt like subtle torture at that age. It was best forgotten, until recently.

During a spell of stress and illnesses a few years ago, I was reintroduced to mindfulness by my physician friend. Though sceptical at first, I did sign up for a package of five classes. The very first class itself was quite comforting from a couple of perspectives. The sheer number of participants in the class conveyed that there was something about it that people valued. In fact, many were regulars and found it to be life-changing. But what really assured me was that the facilitator, Angie Chew, who I mentioned earlier, had been a corporate leader herself before she turned into an advocate of this practice. Hearing from her that I'd come to the right place immediately alleviated all my concerns and fears about this practice.

If you are anything like me, let me first dispel some ambiguities surrounding mindfulness.

- Though originally practised by saints and spiritual leaders, there isn't anything spiritual or mystical about the practice itself. Anyone and everyone can do it.
- Yoga, meditation and mindfulness are interrelated. If yoga is the mother, meditation is her offspring. There are different kinds of meditation. Mindfulness is just one of them. It has many varieties: body scans, love kindness, etc.
- No, it's not about achieving a state of nirvana. It is about being 'mindful' or aware of your 'present' without ascribing any value or judgement to it. Not reading your thoughts as positive or negative, but simply acknowledging them as they are.
- When you focus on the present moment, it helps your thoughts stay put, versus them running away to the past or the future, where our worries and anxieties reside.
- Through a focus on the present, the mind feels calmer. Biologically, your parasympathetic nervous system gets activated. It restores your emotions and makes you feel less stressed and more relaxed.

- You get to decide whether you are doing it right or not. As psychologist Ellen Langer from Harvard said, you are mindful if you start noticing moment-to-moment changes around you, from the different expressions on the face of your spouse across the breakfast table to the variability of your asthma symptoms.[1]

Now, on the other side of this coin is mindlessness. What does that do to us?

Our thoughts are all over the place as the mind spends its time focusing on the past (in regret mode), the future (in worry mode), and trying out should-haves and what-ifs. In a *Harvard Business Review* article, Shawn Achor and Michelle Gielan asserted that if you answer yes to any of the following questions, you may be ready for some mindfulness:[2]

1. When you aren't doing something 'productive', do you feel you are wasting your time or feel guilty?
2. When you don't have meetings, do you fill your time by browsing on your phone or refreshing your inbox?
3. If you have downtime, do you feel lost as to how to fill it?
4. Do you want a more successful team?
5. Do you want a promotion?

According to psychologists Matthew Killingsworth and Daniel Gilbert at Harvard, we spend 47 per cent of our waking hours thinking about something other than what we are doing in the present.[3]

A wandering mind is an unhappy mind, they observed.

So now that we know what mindfulness is and isn't, let's move on to understanding how it benefits us or how it can help us beat burnout and live better.

The benefits

Several studies show that mindfulness is good for us. Shian-Ling Keng and colleagues from Duke University reviewed the empirical literature to understand the effect of mindfulness on our psychological health.[4] Across many studies, they found that it brings about many positive effects. There is improved well-being and reduced emotional reactivity. Specifically, there is less anxiety, depression, anger and perceived stress, and improved behavioural regulation as demonstrated by self-compassion and empathy.

To understand the 'why' behind this, Sofie Valk and others from the Max Planck Institute for Human Cognitive and Brain Sciences, Germany, showed that different kinds of mindfulness practices change and strengthen different areas of the brain. In their study, they engaged participants who were between the ages of twenty and fifty-five years in three different types of training for three months each, totalling a nine-month study period. The first training was referred to as the 'Presence' module. Here, participants learned to focus their attention, bringing it back when it wandered, and to attend to their breathing and internal body sensations. The second was called 'Affect', which sought to enhance empathy and compassion for others; participants learned 'loving kindness' meditation and worked with partners, the goal being to enhance one's compassion and empathy. The last was the 'Perspective' module that focused on observing one's own thoughts non-judgementally and enhancing the understanding of others' perspectives.[5]

The team noted that each of the trainings enhanced different parts of the brain. Presence was linked to increased thickness in the areas that are strongly involved in attention. Affect training was linked to increased thickness in regions known to be involved in socially driven emotions like empathy. Perspective training was associated with changes in areas involved in understanding the mental states of others.

Together, these changes and enhancements pointed to the fact that mindfulness can powerfully boost emotional intelligence and well-being.

Moreover, conscious inhalation and exhalation— slow and long breathing, which is part of the mindfulness practice—aid in regulating emotions by tapping into the parasympathetic nervous system, which is the 'rest and digest' part of the nervous system, the opposite of the 'fight or flight' part. When you breathe slowly and deeply, you start to calm down. Emma Seppala of Stanford University found that army veterans' PTSD (post-traumatic stress disorder) scores normalized within a week of practising breathing and the benefits remained even one year later, suggesting a long-term improvement.[6]

Dr Jyoti Chhabra, a scientist by training and profession, shared, 'I used to feel negative, anxious and stressed. Mindfulness gave me that avenue to release my negativity. I found it calming and healing. As a routine, I practise it every morning and night for fifteen minutes at least. Sometimes I do it when I feel stressed at work—right here in my office.'

So significant are the benefits of mindfulness that tech companies are also adopting it. Not too long ago, Amy Blankson from the Institute of Applied Positive Research ran a pilot study with Google's new hires. The participants were encouraged to practise mindfulness for two minutes a day and maintain a gratitude journal. The result? Engagement scores increased for this intervention group.

Another example is that of Aetna, a large health insurance company, which instituted a mindfulness training programme for its employees.[7] More than a quarter of its 50,000 employees participated in it. On average, stress levels dropped by 28 per cent, reported sleep quality improved by 20 per cent. On the savings front, on average, mindfulness participants gained sixty-two minutes of productivity a week, which Aetna estimated to be worth $3000 per employee per year.

Having established that mindfulness is beneficial, let's turn towards how to practise it.

The practice itself

Like everything else in our world, there are many ways to engage in mindfulness. The simplest and yet most effective I found were the body scan (Presence) and loving-kindness (Affect) mindfulness practices that Angie Chew taught us. A body scan involves mentally scanning every part of your body and being grateful to them. The loving-kindness method invokes a sense of love for yourself and others who have touched your life. Both can be done lying down or sitting, in just ten minutes.

Body-scan mindfulness

Sit in a comfortable position.

Feet touching the ground and back upright.

Close your eyes and take three deep breaths.

Relax as you breathe naturally.

Become aware of the sounds around you.

Accept the sounds and then leave them in the background.

Shift your focus to your body.

Tune into your body to sense how it feels.

Breathe relaxation into any part of the body where you feel tension.

Then drop your attention to your feet.

Starting with your feet, scan your toes, then your calves, and go upwards to your thighs, abdomen, shoulders, neck, arms, chest, face and the top of your head.

If you notice any pain or numbness, embrace it.

Pain is your friend, not a foe, as it warns you to adjust your body or consciously relax.

Now your body is fully relaxed.

Notice where your breath is.

Allow yourself to focus on breathing, on the tip of your nose.

If it helps, count your breaths from 1 to 10, and then count backwards. Repeat as needed, till your mind is able to stay more focused on breathing.

Be kind to your breathing.

If your mind chooses to wander, allow it to do so.

Simply notice your breath again.

Observe three more breaths and very gently open your eyes

You can either go through these steps in your mind on your own or use an audio track to guide you. There are many that you can download from the Internet.

Love-kindness mindfulness

This practice is about loving and appreciating yourself. Psychologist Barbara Fredrickson and colleagues found that seven weeks of doing this practice increased love, joy, contentment, gratitude, pride, hope, interest, amusement and awe among the study participants.[8] It also enhanced a wide range of personal resources such as purpose in life and social support, and decreased illness symptoms, which predicted decreased depressive symptoms and increased life satisfaction and well-being.

To harness its power, sit comfortably, take three deep breaths, and silently say:

'May I be well and happy.'

'May my body be well and healthy.'

Repeat.

These phrases keep you anchored to your body and evoke feelings of love and kindness towards the self. Do this with kindness, especially with a feeling of gratitude towards your body that is carrying you.

At the very foundation, the solution to burnout lies in loving yourself, being humane towards yourself. Mindfulness serves as an avenue to do so.

To integrate mindfulness in your daily schedule, do the following:

- **Two minutes.** As a ritual, when you first get to work in the morning, spend two minutes doing nothing except watching your breath go in and out.
- **Five minutes.** Every night, before going to bed, do a body scan or the love-kindness practice for five minutes.
- **Ten minutes.** If you find the above calming and relaxing, increase the practice to ten minutes or more.

Sitting quietly can be a challenge in the beginning but when you get into the habit you will find it relaxing. Give it a try.

Good relationships with family and friends
are critical for health and well-being

Make time for the important people in your
life

When stressed, double up on their support

14

Double Up on Friends

I MET ONEIL Owens in Singapore. He was then the marketing director for a pharma company, responsible for the Asia region: India, South East Asia, Korea and Japan. I was introduced to him by a common friend who thought we could help each other. I was researching burnout and he was experiencing one.

Oneil was burned out, and trying hard to do damage control. Like many other expatriates, he was swamped supporting Asia during the day and the US at night. As we chatted about his work over a cup of tea in his office, he said, 'You know, I am so glad you stopped by to say hello. I rarely do this kind of thing. I am so busy at work that there is seldom any kind of diversion for me. It would be great if we can meet as a family one of these weekends.' Absolutely, I said, and after a good discussion on burnout, left his office mulling over our conversation.

One of the things that stood out was that he was completely alone. He had no friends or colleagues to turn to, even for a simple chat. He was the senior-most in his office in Singapore, and because of that, his conversations were guarded and limited. Outside of work, he did not have any activity or outlet to release his stress. Though he had a family, he was constantly on calls through the evenings. It was clear that he was keen on bringing about a sense of balance in his life. Perhaps that was why he wanted our families to befriend each other.

There is no doubt that social relationships are critical for our survival. As human beings, we need people around us. We have that inherent need for dependence, support and sharing. This is how communities and societies evolved in the first place—by supporting and protecting each other. In fact, according to Charles Darwin, communities that include the greatest number of sympathetic members flourish best and rear the greatest number of offspring—a sign of thriving.[1]

Relationships, whether with friends, family or others, are one of the most powerful means for eliciting positive emotions and effective recovery. Anyone who has enjoyed a happy family gathering or an evening with good friends knows the profound sense of joy, laughter, safety and security that these relationships bring. We feel blessed to have people around in good times and bad.

In a number of empirical studies, some tracking thousands of people for years, close relationships predicted health and increased feelings of happiness, security and self-worth. When Brigham Young University researcher Julianne Holt-Lunstad and others collated data from 148 studies totalling more than 3,00,000 people globally, they confirmed a striking effect of social support.[2] Those with more connections had survival rates about 50 per cent higher than those with fewer connects. The impact of fewer connections appeared to equal the effect of smoking fifteen cigarettes a day or having an alcohol abuse issue, and double the effect of being obese.

Reinforcing this, another landmark study by Sarah Pressman at the University of California, Irvine, and Sheldon Cohen at Carnegie Mellon University found that more than obesity, drinking and smoking, loneliness reduces longevity by a massive 70 per cent.[3] It is related to psychological stress, poor sleep quality and increased levels of cortisol circulating in our bodies. On the other hand, feelings of social connection strengthen our immune system, lengthen our life, and lower rates of anxiety and depression.

Dan Buettner, a National Geographic fellow and author, did some fascinating research to establish the link between support systems and health.[4] He studied the health habits of those who lived in blue zones: regions of the world where people live way longer than the average. In Okinawa, Japan, where the average life expectancy for women is around ninety, people form a social network called a *moai*: a group of five friends who offer social, logistic, emotional and financial support for a lifetime. He attributed women's longevity to these bonds. Friends can exert a measurable and ongoing influence on your health behaviours in a way that a diet never can, Buettner asserted.

Though we all know the value of relationships, at times we fail to nurture them. We get so busy with work that spending time with loved ones takes a back seat. What we forget is that these very relationships can protect us from the pressures of life. Empirical work shows that those who prioritize relationships along with their work perform better at work.

This came from a study that was conducted as a collaborative effort by three organizations: the Families and Work Institute, Catalyst and Boston College.[5] The authors found that dual-centric employees (who give similar priority to family and work) exhibited greater satisfaction with their jobs and lives and advanced further in their careers than work-centric employees (who focused only on work). They also felt less stressed overall. Around 26 per cent of dual-centric people experienced moderate or high levels of stress compared with 42 per cent who were work-centric.

The findings also showed that dual-centric executives had a much easier time managing both sets of responsibilities. Only 31 per cent, compared to 56 per cent who were not dual-centric, found it difficult to manage both priorities. My guess would be that the dual-centrics were clear about their priorities and hence experienced no confusion in their mind about spending quality time at both places. The work-centrics, on the other hand, likely felt torn making choices between work and family.

When it comes to family relationships, positive and supportive marriages too are key to well-being. A seventy-year study led by George Vaillant at Harvard University found that at age fifty, healthy ageing is better predicted by a good marriage than by low cholesterol levels.[6] Similarly, those in less conflicted marriages lived longer and healthier lives than unmarried individuals, according to a study by psychologists Roger Kaplan and Richard Kronick at the University of California in Los Angeles and San Diego, respectively.[7]

That positive marital relationships offer security and comfort was explored by James Coan of the University of Virginia, and Hillary Schaefer and Richard Davidson of the University of Wisconsin-Madison.[8] They subjected sixteen happily married women to the threat of electronic shock to the ankle as they lay in a functional magnetic resonance imaging (fMRI) machine. During the experiment, some women held their husband's hand, some held the hand of an unknown person or no hand at all. While waiting for the occasional shocks, those who held their husband's hand showed less activity in the brain's threat response areas. This calming benefit was greatest for those who also reported the highest quality marriages. These women felt more secure and drew comfort from their spouse's presence.

So what do these studies tell us? Positive relationships are a source of great comfort and care. They serve as protective shields that help us regulate our emotions. We process our challenges far better when we feel we are not alone. Can you recall a time when you perhaps felt in the dumps but had a spouse or friend to talk to and unburden yourself?

According to Shawn Achor, author of *The Happiness Advantage*, people who survive stress most effectively are the ones who actually increase their social investments in the middle of stress, which is the opposite of what most of us do. When you are busy, you need more friends. In fact, twice as much work means you need friends twice as much, he said. Students who respond to their workload by living in the library and eating meals in their rooms so they can keep studying are the ones who burn out. By not being with others, they cut themselves off from the greatest predictor of happiness which predicts success.[9]

Support from co-workers shows similar results. Feeling valued, supported, respected and socially secure is associated with engagement, productivity and performance. Professors Viswesvaran Chockalingham and colleagues from Florida International University found that social support not only reduces strain, but also diminishes how you perceive the stressors to begin with.[10] Connecting with others gives you the confidence that you can handle challenges.

And the result of feeling socially connected is greater psychological well-being, which translates into higher productivity at work. This is partly because social connectedness leads to higher self-esteem, trust and collaboration.

How is there such a powerful link between support and well-being?

There are many possibilities.

First, family and friends are there to simply give us a hand when we feel low. A listening ear and a warm hug do wonders to our well-being. These gestures help us regulate emotions and prevent us from sliding down into the deep waters of loneliness, depression or bad habits. We process challenges far better when we feel we are not alone. These connects elevate the levels of oxytocin hormones that indirectly inhibit the release of cortisol or the stress hormone. Recall how good you feel when someone gives you a hug when you desperately need one?

Second, sociability gives us an avenue to share and 'get it out' of our system. In a study led by James Pennebaker, thirty-three Holocaust survivors spent one or two hours talking about their experience, recalling and sharing details with their families and friends. Those who shared more had a better health status fourteen months later. According to the author, confiding in someone helps release pent-up emotions, which instantly makes you feel better. It also stimulates bonding, strengthens social ties and aids in emotional recovery.[11]

Third, those interactions allow us to seek empathy that can instil security and a sense of assurance in us. Bernard Rime at the department of psychology, University of Louvain, Belgium, and colleagues explained this through 'atypical' situations, such as bereavement and other kinds of loss. They observed that empathy, as a result of connectedness, gives people the strength and confidence that they are not alone in this, that 'this too shall pass'.[12]

Fourth, and as mentioned above, connectedness heightens self-esteem, trust and the collaborative spirit; this plays out positively for our well-being.

Clearly, there is a lot riding on our social relationships. Oneil, whom I met in Singapore, purposefully went about widening his network of relationships. Here's what he did:

- On the family front, he committed to two uninterrupted dinners at home.
- He set up one special evening a month with his spouse.
- Every Friday night he went out for dinner with the family.
- On the weekend, he made it a practice to call on friends he had lost touch with.
- At work, he had a standing commitment every Wednesday to have lunch with a colleague.
- He joined his apartment's basketball team.

To build your relationships, you can implement similar practices:

- **Make it a priority.** Put it on your calendar. Schedule time for your friends, family and colleagues just as you would for your work commitments. Make weekly or monthly standing engagements.
- **Carve out family time.** There are several ways to strengthen your relationship with your partner, children or extended family. Simple things like having dinner together, doing dishes, running errands, dropping kids to school, or playing a board game or cards can open up avenues to spend time together. Create family rituals, such as taking one or two family vacations a year, a movie night with popcorn every Friday, or date nights once a month with your spouse. For long-distance relationships, leverage technology. Use video chat to wish them on their special days or to simply talk. Seeing and chatting enables a stronger connect than talking or texting.
- **Spend time with friends.** Seek more support, especially when stressed. Watch movies, go out on walks or hikes, exercise together or simply hang out for a good laugh. While Facebook or WhatsApp chats are great, true value and connections happen only through personal interactions. Remember, online friends can't hug you when a crisis hits, visit you when you're sick, or celebrate a happy occasion with you in person.
- **Get to know your colleagues.** Schedule coffee or lunch breaks with them. Considering you spend most of your time at work, it's a great place to strike up friendships (barring conflicts of interest). Your colleagues can not only be good sounding boards for your work-related issues, but as you get to know them better, for personal conversations as well.

- **Ask for help.** A key to building and maintaining relationships is to show your vulnerability. Brené Brown, professor at the University of Houston Graduate College of Social Work, in her book *Daring Greatly* shows that when we allow ourselves to be seen as vulnerable— when we admit our fears or self-doubt—we connect better.[13] In sharing our fears and insecurities, we find true relationships, as research by James Pennebaker also suggests. So you don't always have to be that furiously independent, strong person. Let your guard down for a true connection to happen.

- **Give.** It cultivates care, trust and cooperative behaviour. Be a good friend. Listen and help. Mentor, volunteer, share your resources, and engage in extracurricular activities. They not only make great avenues to cultivate relationships, but also enhance your sense of accomplishment, as plenty of research shows. I will share more on this in the next chapter.

All these practices help regulate emotions. Spending time with others can reduce stress and nurture well-being.

Acts of gratitude and generosity do the following:

1) Lower stress and the incidence of burnout
2) Enhance well-being
3) Yield better performance and success

15

Be Grateful and Give Back

R ESEARCH SHOWS THAT we have more positive experiences than negative ones, yet we have a greater tendency to focus on the negative aspects of our lives. We take the good things for granted and blow up the unpleasant ones. With the result that we sweat the small stuff, letting it hijack our well-being.

Only when we look at others who have faced significant adversities do we begin to realize how minor our daily annoyances actually are.

How can we change our lens to capitalize on what we have instead of letting what we don't have rule our well-being?

By showing gratitude, being thankful for what we have, and being sharing and giving with others, suggests empirical evidence.

When psychologists Robert Emmons of the University of California, Davis, and Michael McCullough of the University of Miami wanted to explore the relationship between gratitude and well-being, they asked the participants to write a few sentences each week, focusing on particular topics.[1] One group wrote about things they were grateful for that had occurred during the week. A second group wrote about daily irritants or things that had bothered them, and a third wrote about events that had affected them. The finding was that after ten weeks, those who wrote about gratitude were not only more optimistic and felt better about their lives, but also healthier than those who focused on sources of irritation.

In another endeavour, psychologist Philip Watkins and colleagues from Eastern Washington University had participants engage in one of three experimental conditions: (a) thinking about someone to whom they felt grateful; (b) writing about someone to whom they felt grateful; or (c) writing a letter to someone to whom they felt grateful.[2] All three of these experimental conditions led to greater short-term increases in positive affect and appreciation, and greater short-term reductions in negative emotions—complaining or feeling like a victim—than a control condition did (such as writing about the layout of one's living room).

In similar vein, psychologist Martin Seligman at the University of Pennsylvania looked at the impact of various positive psychology interventions on well-being and how they compared with the control group of participants.[3] When their week's assignment was to write and personally deliver a letter of gratitude to someone who had never been properly thanked for their kindness, participants immediately exhibited a huge increase in happiness scores. This impact was greater than that from any other intervention, with benefits lasting up to thirty days.

What is it about gratitude that reduces stress and heightens our well-being?

Evidently, the act of appreciation or being thankful stimulates two important regions in our brain: the one that regulates stress and the one that activates the brain's reward system and evokes feelings of pleasure.

Research shows that gratitude also induces feelings of giving or serving others. When we feel happy and enjoy the benefits of others' gestures and blessings, we want to reciprocate or pass them on to others. In other words, being thankful makes us want to give. And when we give, we feel happy and so does the recipient. The act of giving actually ties back to our evolutionary heritage, where the give and take of resources generated critical interactions for survival. It reflected a symbiotic relationship then, and it continues to be so today as well.

Spending money on others can make us happy too. Michael Norton of Harvard Business School conducted a series of studies with his colleagues Elizabeth Dunn and Lara Aknin of the University of British Columbia.[4] Together they showed that people are happier when they spend money on others versus on themselves. In their experiment, they handed envelopes of money to students on campus. The recipients were told they should spend the money (either $5 or $20) by the end of that day either on themselves or on others, as a gift or a donation to charity. The results showed that irrespective of the amount, people who spent the money on themselves that day weren't happier that evening. But those who spent it on others were.

Giving or generosity is a powerful source of well-being. It is linked with better health. A study led by Ashley Whillans, psychologist at the University of British Columbia, and colleagues found that the more money people spent on others, the lower their blood pressure was two years later.[5] Giving stimulates the reward areas in the brain that helps to create positive feelings by reducing stress. Additionally, it gives us a sense of purpose and heightens feelings of self-worth.

Geoff Turk finds giving an excellent stress buster. 'Helping or appreciating others directs the focus away from you to others, because of which you forget your own challenges. You recognize you are so blessed and that you are in a good position to make a difference in others' lives.' He added, 'After I got involved in volunteering, I realized how petty my work problems were compared to others'. Performance reviews and promotions didn't matter at all. I felt more satisfied and fulfilled giving my time and love to those who needed me. In a way, I am grateful for all the stress I incurred at work; that's what pushed me towards volunteering in the first place.'

Gratitude and giving go hand in hand and make you reflective, appreciative and grounded.

So how do we incorporate gratitude and giving into our lives?

Here are some research-backed insights relating to gratitude:

1. **Keep a gratitude journal.** Several studies have found that with repeated action, you can rewire your brain in as little time as three weeks. By keeping a gratitude journal and writing in it frequently you can rewire your brain to actually experience more gratitude. As you notice the positives, you will automatically notice lesser negatives.[6]

   Leadership coach Robin Sharma suggests journaling every morning. Write down a list of things you are grateful for: I have food on the table, I am healthy, I have a great family, I am making a positive difference in others' lives, etc. This activity releases serotonin and dopamine, enhancing productivity, focus and quality of life.[7]

2. **Enjoy the moment.** Don't postpone joy or happiness. Relish what you have. Share your good news with co-workers and friends; it will create a sense of belonging and attachment with them and help guard against burnout. Slow down to truly feel and appreciate the present moment. Be mindful of your surroundings; it will give you a sense of awe and wonder that's known to trigger good chemicals in the body.

3. **Write a thank-you note.** Express your enjoyment and appreciation of a person's impact on your life or work. Not only will you feel good, so will the recipient of your praise.

And here's how you can give:

1. **Make a choice.** Identify the direction in which you want to give. Is there any particular cause you feel strongly about? Being intentional will serve as a filter to disburse your money and time.

2. **Make time.** Besides giving money, volunteering your time and expertise can be as fulfilling or more. If education is your passion, go teach in a school, spend time with children, share your knowledge and make learning fun. Offer your expertise pro bono. For example, you can help social organizations improve their existing processes or implement new systems to better their efficiencies. At work, mentor employees and share your experience with them.

   Again, carve out this time on your calendar.

3. **Do random acts of kindness.** Allocate a fixed sum of money to share with those who are working hard. Consider it a responsibility to give others a helping hand. Buy lunch for a friend, help someone cross the road, or offer to carry someone's grocery bags. The sky is the limit if you just slow down a tad to make others happy. According to Matthieu Ricard, the author of *Altruism*, ask yourself: Would I be just as happy if someone else performed this act of kindness.[8] If yes, engage in those deeds. 'For a true altruist, it's the result that counts, not the personal satisfaction of having helped,' he observed.

4. **Be a good friend or colleague.** Lend an ear when someone needs it. Be compassionate and supportive. If you see

someone feeling low, perk them up by talking to them or taking them out.

Acts of gratitude and giving can measurably reduce levels of cortisol in our bodies. What is stopping you from engaging in them?

Smile and laugh; they lower stress

Engage in activities and interactions that tickle you

16

Smile and Laugh

AN EFFORTLESS WAY to alter our mood and get rid of stress is to simply smile and laugh. Even if the acts are not genuine!

One of my good friends, Nita, has an ever-smiling face. So much so that everyone refers to her as the smiling lady. Her smile is wondrous; it brings a positive affect and lightens the ambience in seconds.

Some people do have that kind of an effect. There are many studies that associate smiling with feel-good outcomes for the self and others. It has been linked with happiness, social connection, strong marriages, health, longevity, attractiveness and enhanced well-being.

Several experiments have subtly induced participants to feel different emotions such as anger, fear and happiness just by asking them to stretch or contract their facial muscles. It is called the facial feedback effect wherein those tiny muscles can trigger corresponding emotions in us. For example, when you force yourself to smile at a social event, you will actually come to find the event more enjoyable. On the other hand, if you frown, you are bound to find the experience lousy.

To avoid stress and fatigue, a quick way to perk up is to smile. It reduces the intensity of the stress response. Tara Kraft from the University of Kansas and Sarah Pressman from the University of California, Irvine, studied how different types of smiling and awareness of smiling can affect one's ability to recover from stress.[1] In their experiment, they found that compared to individuals who held neutral expressions, those who were instructed to smile, and in particular those with genuine smiles, had lower heart rate levels after recovery from stressful activities. This was because smiling diminished cortisol production in their bodies.

Interestingly enough, how we smile in pictures is also indicative of our well-being. LeeAnne Harker and Dacher Keltner from the University of California, Berkeley, looked at college yearbook photos to test this hypothesis.[2] At the time the yearbook photos were taken—when the women were about twenty-one years old—the more they were smiling in their photos, the more they said they felt a sense of well-being. What was more interesting was that they reported greater well-being at ages twenty-seven, forty-three and fifty-two (when the researchers followed up).

More recently, Patrick Seder and Shigehiro Oishi from the University of Virginia explored something very similar.[3] They collected Facebook profile pictures from first-semester college students. Similar to the study mentioned above, those who smiled more in their profiles during their first semester reported greater life satisfaction 3.5 years later.

What's more, some creative researchers tested the impact of botox (which paralyses the frown muscles) on well-being. Here's what they found. Eric Finzi from Dermatology and Cosmetic Surgery Associates, Maryland, and Erika Wasserman noted that nine out of ten of their depressed patients felt better after they were given between-the-eyebrows botox injections.[4] In another experiment, Michael Lewis at the University of Cardiff in Wales found that because of botox, those who were unable to frown and express negative emotions facially had significantly less negative moods. They reported feeling happier and less anxious in general.[5] Conclusively, then, botox isn't bad after all: it smoothes out life's emotional wrinkles too!

Smiling is contagious. Just as it gives us a good feel, it also evokes smiles from others. In a Swedish study conducted by Marianne Sonnby–Borgström, subjects were shown pictures of several emotions: joy, anger, fear and surprise. When the picture of someone smiling was presented, the researchers asked the subjects to frown. They couldn't. Instead, their facial expressions imitated what they saw. It took deliberate effort to turn that smile upside-down.[6] The reason for this is that we have mirror neurons that fire when we see action. They allow us to copy or reflect the behaviour we observe in others. We yawn when we see someone yawning. Our faces express sadness when we see someone sad. The same is the case with smiling. When we see others smile at us, we automatically smile back.

Given these findings, a simple antidote for burnout is to smile as much as you can. Even if you are not genuinely happy, just the act of smiling turns on your brain receptors to produce dopamine and serotonin: the feel-good neurotransmitters that work towards combating stress. They not only make you feel brighter, but also open up the learning centres of the brain, allowing you to be more flexible and creative in your thinking as well as enhancing your ability to effectively process information.

Ron Gutman, the author of *Smile: The Astonishing Powers of a Simple Act*, recommends we should smile over twenty times a day at least (children smile over 400 times).[7]

If smiling has so much power, laughter has it too. A joke, a comedy show or anything humorous can have us in splits. At least in that particular moment, we feel better. In a small study conducted by Gurinder Bains at Loma Linda University in Southern California, twenty normal, healthy, older adults watched a funny video distraction-free for twenty minutes, while another control group sat silently with no video or any other distraction.[8] Afterwards, they performed memory tests and had their saliva samples analysed for stress hormones. You guessed it. Those who got to laugh the twenty minutes away with the funny video scored better on short-term memory tests. Also, the stress hormone cortisol had significantly decreased in the humour group.

Laughter as therapy is also quite effective. Psychologists Anuja Deshpande from Maniben Nanavati Women's College and Vaishnavi Verma from Smt MMP Shah Women's College of Arts and Commerce, both in Mumbai, tested the impact of laughter therapy on happiness and life satisfaction among the elderly.[9] They found that laughter therapy had a positive impact on their participants. Those who had undergone therapy for six months showed a higher sense of well-being and happiness than those without the laughter intervention.

Research also shows that laughter can aid in the recovery of heart patients. Work referenced in a paper by Michael Balick and Roberta Lee showed that among heart patients, of those who were prescribed thirty minutes of laughter per day, only 8 per cent of those suffered a second heart attack.[10] This was in contrast to 40 per cent in the control group. Laughter worked to improve cardiovascular conditioning.

According to Lee Berk, the co-author of the California study referenced above, laughter or humour reduces stress hormones and lowers blood pressure. It enhances our mood state by increasing endorphins and sending dopamine to the brain, which strengthen the immune system for better health.

For Raghu, who was the chief HR officer at GE and recently retired after twenty-five years of service, laughter is the best medicine. 'Every night before going to bed, I have to take my dose of laughter. Without fail, I watch a comedy show. Those few minutes of unrestrained laughter unwind and destress me.'

A colleague of mine follows a different ritual. Every morning, during his walk, he meets a group of people who practise the laughter exercise. They laugh out loud for about ten minutes, oxygenating their bodies. 'It is such a wonderful feeling to laugh it all out. All the negativity and toxins get released. You feel light. Just as importantly, it is great fun!'

If you haven't guessed it, laughter is also infectious. It brings people together and increases happiness and closeness. To enhance your well-being do the following:

- **Engage in fun activities and laugh out loud.** Watch funny movies or shows, read comics and jokes, play with a pet, go to a laughter yoga class, do something silly.
- **Tell yourself to smile and laugh more.** Is your commute a pain, or are you fed up of doing dishes or chores? Paste on a smile as you go about doing them. The sheer act of smiling and laughing will perk you up.
- **Smile at others.** Whether in the elevator, at the cash register or somewhere else, smile. The mirror neurons will make others smile too!

Reflection Points

1. Emotions are the bedrock of well-being. By training to dial down the flight–fight system, situations can be handled better.
2. Techniques of reframing, STOP, visualization and power posing can foster emotional stability and lower the incidence of burnout.
3. Mindfulness facilitates focusing on the 'present' moment without any judgement. It prevents ruminating over the past and worrying about the future.
4. Friends, family and colleagues form an excellent support system to keep burnout at bay.
5. Gratitude and giving gestures lower stress and enhance well-being.
6. Smiling and laughing, even if not genuine, are cathartic stress-relievers.

Mental Focus

Work Smart: The Ten Pillars for Building Efficiencies

1) Write your to-do list
2) Plan your day according to your energy levels
3) Work the calendar
4) Email at planned hours
5) Manage your meetings
6) Say no
7) Delegate and outsource
8) Take a break every 90 minutes
9) Keep the phone away
10) Take time off

17

Work Smart: The Ten Pillars for Building Efficiencies

THE IMAGINATION CAN run wild. Mine does too.

When I am swamped, I have often visualized myself as a little puppy running round and round in circles. Huffing and puffing, I am on the go, working hard, creating a dust cloud around me, thinking I am doing well. But when I stop, there is no treat or reward waiting for me. Because even though I've done a lot of running, there has been no definite progress. I have nothing concrete to show for it. All I've accomplished is to exhaust my energies in doing 'something'.

Pressing deadlines, expectations, meetings, presentations and pleasing stakeholders day in and day out can make us go in circles, rendering us incapable of functioning effectively.

This brings us to the third level of the Well-being State Pyramid: enhancing our mental focus so we can avoid creating dust clouds around us. By introducing efficiencies in our work, we can channel our energies and focus for better outcomes. We can have a perfect day—advance towards our legacy, complete our to-do lists, and go home to spend quality time with our families, all without getting unduly stressed or anxious.

Here are the ten pillars of working smart that I and many others have leveraged to enable progress and keep burnout at bay:

1. Write your to-do list
2. Plan your day according to your energy levels
3. Work the calendar
4. Email at planned hours
5. Manage your meetings
6. Say no
7. Delegate and outsource
8. Take a break every ninety minutes
9. Keep the phone away
10. Take time off

Let's look at each of them to see how doing them right can preserve our energies, build efficiencies and set us free to truly focus on things that matter to us. All without compromising our health, relationships or well-being.

Write your to-do list

Old-fashioned as it may be, the to-do list can be a lifesaver. It gives you a complete glimpse of what needs to be done and helps you script your day in advance.

To use it effectively, put down on paper everything you need to do (writing allows a quicker connection with the brain than typing). List out the emails you need to send, calls you have to make, who you have to meet, presentations to be completed, errands to be run, gym sessions, etc. Personally, this task can be highly motivating as you see the many opportunities you have to make a difference. It can get the adrenaline going, creating a rush of positive stress or eustress flowing through your body for optimal performance.

Once you have everything listed, prioritize. Circle the things that are absolutely critical to be accomplished today. Filter out those that can wait or be delegated. Next, rank-order the shortlist. What needs to be done first, second, third and so forth. For that matter, there could be interdependencies too: task three on the list could require you to finish task one first.

You get the drift?

Next, make your to-do list visible. Write it down on a bright notepad and keep that in front of you so you look at it often. This will serve as a reminder for all the things you need to be working on that day.

Additionally, slot these tasks in your calendar. Allocate time to each of them, along with the start and end times. Predefined windows can make you mentally prepared about how much time you need to spend on each task. It also forces you to focus and be highly effective. In the absence of these boundaries, you can easily get carried away doing just your first task. Parkinson's Law captures the essence of this behaviour. It shows that we have a tendency to use up all the time in the absence of a deadline. So, if you have a 5 p.m. deadline, you will work until 5 p.m. If you have a 2 p.m. deadline you will get the same amount of work done by that time. In other words, work can expand to fill the available time at hand. To work smart, set time boundaries for yourself. Of course, this may pose a challenge and not be as effective if you are engaged in creative or innovative tasks.

As you complete your tasks, be sure to cross them off your list one by one. Seeing your list shrink can keep you excited and motivated to get through the day.

Plan your day according to your energy levels

Perhaps the most common advice you have heard is to schedule your most important tasks in the morning when you are at your freshest. I've heard it too. While there is some truth to it, not everyone is at their best during those early hours. Some are groggy and actually too tired then to be able to deliver their best.

Our productivity depends on our unique chronotype or internal clock. One that impacts what time of the day we are most focused, creative, in a good mood, or likely to make mistakes.

According to Daniel Pink,[1] we experience three productivity phases through the course of the day: peak, trough, and rebound or recovery. For most of us, our peaks are in the mornings and evenings. Between lunch and the end of the workday is the trough: our lowest point of the day aside from when we wake up. In light of this, it is best to leverage our peaks for analytical tasks (strategizing, analysing, writing), our troughs for administrative or routine tasks such

Circadian Rhythm

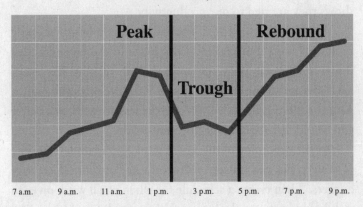

Source: https://zapier.com/blog/chronotype-productivity-schedule

as making phone calls or sending emails, and the rebound phase for creative activities.

While the peaks and troughs are consistent across the population, their timings can vary. For some, the peak can happen in the evening and nights instead of in the morning. It is dependent on our individual biological clocks. Pink identified three types of chronotypes: lark, third bird, and owl.

Larks are the morning people. Irrespective of work, they are out and about in the morning. They wake up before 7 a.m.

Third birds make the most common chronotype—about 65 per cent of the population. They like to wake up between 8–10 a.m.

Owls are night people. They sleep late and don't get up until after 10 a.m.

While larks and third birds experience their day in a peak, trough and recovery sequence, night owls experience their day in reverse: recovery, trough and peak.

Why is it important for us to know these phases? Evidence shows they are tied to our productivity.

As a lark or a third bird, you will be more productive doing analytical tasks that require acute focus in the morning. But if you are an owl, then you are better off making important decisions and doing analytical work in the evenings and nights. And the more productive you are, the less stressed and better you would feel about managing your work.

At the beginning of the day or week, get an understanding of your tasks and cluster them into analytical and creative buckets. Then create a schedule for when you'll work on each task based on your chronotype. Now, in the event you find your tasks are both analytical and creative, parse your tasks and focus more on what aligns with your internal clock at that time of the day. For example, to make a presentation for your stakeholders, focus on the actual data and thoughtful insights during your peak hours and on its creative presentation side during the recovery phase. This is not to say you cannot do the two together. Creativity too can require deep thinking at times. The separation of analytical and creative tasks is only a guiding principle and can be effectively practised when you have distinctively defined tasks.

Depending on your chronotype, leverage these tactics to build your schedule to maximize your productivity.

Work the calendar

Thank god for the calendar tool! It has made our lives so much simpler. It gives a complete picture of what is going on for you today, tomorrow or the week and beyond.

Once a week, do a 'waste walk' of your calendar to assess which meetings are critical and which ones can be delegated or declined. This little ritual will not only give you a quick preview of what the week ahead looks like, but also a sense of which meetings don't necessarily align with your goals or won't add any value. Weed them out and politely delegate or decline. And the ones that are important get a head start. Ask for the agenda or any pre-work that you can get going with.

One of the things that can make you efficient is to absolutely integrate your personal commitments into this calendar. Whether it is family vacations, kids' activities or something else, mark them in the beginning of the year itself. The next set of professional priorities can then be fitted around them. Sure, things can change, but at least you have a starting point to proceed from. Besides these, leverage the tool to integrate your exercise schedule, doctor appointments and other personal commitments. This will not only serve as a reminder, but also keep others informed about your whereabouts.

Put a 'hold' or block your calendar for critical quiet work. At times, it is impossible to get an uninterrupted window to work on your projects. For that, block a couple of hours on your calendar. This way, anyone looking to schedule a meeting would not overlay anything on that time slot. Moreover, instead of working on those tasks at your desk if you are in an open office layout, take your work to a conference room. You will avoid the interruptions of people, the phone and other distractions.

I find this tactic extremely helpful. To focus on critical projects that require uninterrupted attention, I block a chunk of two hours in the morning and lock myself in a conference room, away from my desk. Not only am I fresh and alert at this time of the day, I can also get the challenging task out of the way first thing in the morning. Blocking a couple of hours in the evening for family time is as helpful. Again, the idea is to prevent other work surfacing during your personal time.

Email at planned hours

There was a time when getting emails was a morale booster. In our heart of hearts, we loved emails for they made us feel important. The sound of a new mail dropping into our inbox excited us. It was a connection; someone needed us. Remember those days?

Today, that isn't the case. According to Eric Garton, a partner in Bain and Company, senior executives today receive over 200 emails a day.[2] The average frontline supervisor devotes about eight hours each week to sending, reading and answering emails. As if that isn't revealing enough, a Microsoft study by Shamsi Iqbal and Eric Horvitz found that it takes people an average of fifteen minutes to return to their task after an email interruption.[3] Given the number of emails that fall into our inbox every second, you only have to calculate the time you lost responding to each.

To avoid such distractions and minimize stress, seek control over your inbox.

As a first, remove notification alerts so your inbox doesn't call you. Technology is for your convenience, not the other way around. You may have withdrawal symptoms at first, but you will soon learn to enjoy the silence.

One of the things that works wonderfully for Rishi, a manager at a health company, is to check mail only at designated times during the day. He has four such slots: in the morning, after lunch, before leaving for home, and before ending his day. He shared, 'I dedicate twenty minutes to each slot, which equals eighty minutes a day. And when I open my inbox, I first look at those mails that are critical for the work I am doing or from my boss. On weekends, I look at my mail once a day in the afternoon. As a practice, I don't send out mails to anyone on weekends.'

If you are new to the company or starting out in your career, and if you agree with this ritual, set your expectations with your boss and peers. They will not only respect your time management, but may also replicate the same in their work protocol.

Now, once you have opened your inbox, do it right the first time. If you open a mail, act on it. Do not close it, telling yourself that you will respond later when you have more time to think through it. It works sometimes, but most of the times, it ends up piling up on your to-do list. So, if you open a mail, do one of the following: respond, delete or file it, suggests Bob Pozen, a senior lecturer of business administration at Harvard Business School and author of *Extreme Productivity*.[4] Get over with that email then and there itself to avoid procrastination.

Keep your response to mails to the point. Avoid wasting time on writing long, winding mails and making others waste time by reading them. Brevity is effective and efficient. The more you minimize your energy spend, the more resources you'll have for tasks that actually matter. Sometimes, picking up the phone and clarifying something is better than starting a never-ending chain of emails.

Resist the urge to hit 'reply all' for correspondence such as 'thank you' mails. One of my colleagues was known for this. This habit of his used to drive so much unwanted traffic that at times it was simply funny for we were all prepared for it. And we are humans after all. When one person says thanks to another in a 'reply all' mail, you too feel the obligation to reciprocate. You give in and soon the floodgates open for a flurry of thanks until everyone has done their part!

Finally, and most importantly, to avoid getting stressed, don't read mails first thing in the morning or when going to bed. They are notorious for ruining our moods and sleep. I am sure, like me, at some point you too have experienced this pain.

Manage your meetings

Ever been in meetings agitating over 'Why are we talking about this?', 'How does this even solve our problem?', 'We are already ten minutes over the scheduled meeting time, when will it end?', 'I am getting late to my next one', or 'I have so much to do and here we are wasting time'?

Ineffective meetings are not only annoying and unproductive, but also a significant drain on the company's resources and ours.

To work smartly and maximize your time, plan your meetings. This begins with having a clear agenda and inviting the right participants to it. Clearly lay out the objective of the meeting, who is responsible for what, and what outcomes are to be expected. If there is any pre-work, send it out in advance so that everyone is prepared and can make useful contributions. Not only do these few tasks offer a structure, they also pump up the participants to add value.

If you are the moderator, keep the discussion on track. If ideas come up, park them away to be addressed later, time permitting. End the meeting on time, but before you adjourn, recap the discussion or any decisions made, and share the action items or next steps as the case may be. In other words, ensure a clean closure.

Say no

One of my colleagues, in her enthusiasm to show initiative and climb the ladder, as has been drummed into women, used to accept every job doled out to her. Unfortunately, this habit of hers slowed her down on her own deliverables and totally consumed her. Imagine your cup is already full and you pour in some more; what happens? It overflows and then you spend more time cleaning it all up.

Early in my career, I too had this disease. In team meetings, when my boss would say he needed a volunteer to drive an initiative, when no one said yes, I would feel compelled to break the silence and raise my hand. But after a point I learned my lesson. When I absolutely didn't have the bandwidth, I would raise my hand and say, 'I would love to take this on, but as you know, my cup is already so full that I won't be able to do justice to this important task.'

There, done, and nicely too!

Another area where saying no becomes important is declining meetings. If a meeting gets scheduled during your family time in the evening, let the invitee know you have a time conflict and won't be able to participate because of your other commitment. To show your interest, do request them to send the meeting minutes and any action items you may be accountable for. Now, this strategy may not always be easy to practise, especially if it's a standing weekly meeting or one set up by your seniors. But here as well, I find that when you do explain your situation or suggest an alternative time, people are quite receptive and understanding.

Remember, burnout tends to hit the best employees and those who promptly accept additional responsibilities. Practise filtering demands and saying no to those that don't align with your goals.

Delegate and outsource

Some of us are extremely possessive about our work. We hold it tight to our chests, wanting to do everything ourselves, our way. This is despite having the support of resources which can share the load. There are many reasons for this kind of behaviour. For one, we believe we are the best, that no one can do it as well as we can. Two, we may not trust someone else to do the task; we worry about quality or timely delivery. Three, we don't want to share the visibility or limelight that may come from doing that piece of work. And finally, we just don't know how to let go.

All this is good if you can manage it without hiccups. But if you can't, and are overwhelmed with the load, unable to focus on critical things and stressed at all times, it's time you let go.

Practise delegating small tasks to test the waters. See if your subordinate can do them on their own. Set clear expectations, timelines, deliverables and feedback paths. Once confident, delegate more. You would be unburdening yourself as well as skilling your team for bigger responsibilities. This is similar to garnering the mastery of experiences that we talked about earlier, in the section on accountability.

On the other hand, if you are short of resources, ask for help. Share the facts with your boss that highlight the business case of why you need additional resources. Meanwhile, hold off on the task, delay the timeline or take something else off your list until you get the support.

Just as you delegate at work, delegate at home as well. Divide tasks among family members so the load is shared. Whether it is doing laundry, buying groceries or cleaning, a clear assignment can save time for all concerned. Encourage children to do chores around the house. You would be nurturing values of independence, responsibility and accountability in them. The more hands at work, the more free time to spend together.

In situations where you still have some tasks to be done or some you absolutely don't enjoy doing, consider outsourcing them. Transactional chores such as house cleaning, cutting grass or cooking are some such examples that can be outsourced. In one of our conversations Marshall Goldsmith said, 'If you are a professional, you shouldn't be spending your time on such chores. Your value-add isn't in tasks that someone else can easily do for you. Your focus should be on utilizing your intellect on things that others cannot do.' I agree with him. This is all the more critical for women who tend to strive towards doing it all.

Outsourcing requires a mindset shift because it takes away control and also costs money. You feel less in control, are dependent on someone else, and feel the sting of paying for tasks that you can easily do yourself. But despite all this, recognize that time has huge value. That's what you are trying to buy by outsourcing.

To ease into this process, create a list of things you don't like doing and view as not worthy of your time. Depending on the size of your pocket, decide what you'd like to outsource. Exercise due diligence to find the right worker to take on that job.

Treat this expense as an investment in your career and well-being. Utilize the free time for better experiences: be with your family, rest or engage in activities you enjoy doing.

Learn to delegate, outsource and let go.

Take a break every ninety minutes

I used to make fun of my spouse and my younger daughter about their work styles. Both of them would work for an hour but follow that up with thirty-minute breaks. I never understood it. I would question how they could be tired in just an hour. Especially when I could slog for many hours at a stretch without any breaks.

But I gained an appreciation for their routine after I stumbled upon research that highlighted the necessity of taking frequent, timely and longer-than-five-minute breaks. Alejandro Lleras and Atsunori Ariga of the University of Illinois conducted a study where they tested participants' ability to focus on a repetitive computerized task for about an hour under different conditions.[5] They found that most participants' performance declined significantly over the course of the task. However, those in a group that took two brief breaks from their main task showed no drop in their performance. Taking breaks allowed them to stay focused during the entire experiment.

What the study demonstrated was that the brain is built to detect and respond to change. It gradually stops registering sights, sounds or feelings if the stimulus remains constant over a period of time. Brief diversions allow the brain to recharge, which improves focus and enhances productivity. The team suggested that when faced with long tasks—such as studying before a final exam or doing your taxes—it is best to impose brief breaks on yourself. They will actually help you stay focused.

As to what is the optimum window for peak performance before productivity begins to wane, here too research comes to our rescue. It suggests that working somewhere in the range of fifty to ninety minutes is optimal. In 1960s, physiologist Nathaniel Kleitman and his research assistant Eugene Aserinsky discovered the rest–activity cycle—called the ultradian cycle—that lasts ninety/twenty minutes (ninety minutes of activity followed by twenty minutes of rest during the day).[6] At night, when you are asleep, it changes to ninety minutes of rest and twenty minutes of activity.

Given this biological programming, our attention begins to fade as we approach the ninety-minute mark. The signals of yawning, hunger and difficulty concentrating begin to surface, telling us to take a break. To restore energy, research suggests taking a twenty-minute break at the ninety-minute mark.

Similar results were highlighted by Jessica Gifford from the Draugiem Group, a research entity.[7] She found that the most productive people worked for fifty-two minutes at a time, then took a break for seventeen minutes before getting back to it.

So, whether it is a 52:17 or 90:20 period, the idea is to not work incessantly, but to alternate between activity and rest cycles that range anywhere from eighty to 120 minutes in total.

Having understood the optimum period for sustained performance, what is so special about taking a break?

According to psychotherapist Ernest Rossi, author of *The 20-minute Break*, during a break, the mind–body resynchronizes the many rhythms and systems.[8] The body works to clear up the oxidative waste products and free radical molecules that have built up in the tissues during previous periods of performance and stress. It is during this downtime that the mind–body communication channels are replenished and energy reserves are restored. On the psychological front, the mind works to make sense of and integrate the day's experiences thus far. Past experiences, feelings and events are synthesized into a coherent whole, creating new levels of meaning and understanding.

Given these findings, unplug and train to take breaks. If a ninety-minute period of uninterrupted work is too much, start with fifty minutes at a time and follow up with a ten-minute break. Find out what window works best for you. Use a timer if needed. And when on a break, stay away from stressful stimuli. Consider doing the following when on a break:

- Stretch
- Close your eyes
- Listen to music
- Take a walk
- Look outside
- Talk to someone
- Do something mundane
- Do nothing

Counterintuitively, idleness can make a great productivity tool. It can stimulate creativity and day-dreaming, suggest psychologists Sandi Mann and Rebekah Cadman of the University of Central Lancashire.[9] Practising this may be uncomfortable initially, just like exercise. But with time and effort you will come to enjoy the idleness.

Keep the phone away

Phones can be saviours or major distractors, depending on how we choose to use them. As the former, they offer us limitless flexibility. We can work from anywhere, respond to emails, draft communications, get on to meetings, stay in touch with our families, and simply free up our time by leveraging the many efficiencies they offer at our fingertips.

Likewise, they come in handy during break times. Taking short smartphone breaks can actually enhance our well-being, contingent upon what you are doing, asserts Sooyeol Kim of Kansas State University. By interacting with friends or family members or by playing a short game, you can recover from some of your stress to refresh your mind.[10] It can improve workplace productivity, make employees happier and benefit businesses. Of course, playing for long durations would only hurt their work performance and deliverables. With moderation as the key, smartphone micro-breaks can keep your stress and focus in check.

On the flip side, though, phones present an extraordinary challenge in keeping our boundaries and focus intact. You look at your phone for a minute, and pretty soon, without realizing it, you are sucked into the vortex of an unending information abyss. It has an incredible knack for taking over your temptations and control. The result? You end up wasting time and energy, delaying your progress, and stressing yourself in the process.

Like Pavlovian dogs, we make associations between the phone and our psychological needs for autonomy, connection and thirst for information. Worse, the mere presence of the smartphone, even when you are not on it, can be distracting enough to impact our functioning, say Adrian Ward and colleagues at the University of Texas, Austin.[11] They found that participants who had their phones in a different room significantly outperformed those with phones on their desk, and slightly outperformed those who had kept their phones in a pocket or bag. The visibility of a smartphone impairs cognitive functioning, even though we feel we are giving our full attention to the task at hand.

Further, the mere sight of the phone also raises cortisol levels in our bodies that immediately trigger physiological changes such as spikes in blood pressure and heart rate that help us react to and survive acute physical threats. All this is good when we are in real danger. But when that's not the case, this release has a negative impact. Phone-induced cortisol spikes are unhealthy, especially when we are on our phones constantly. A recent Google study by Juie Aranda and Safia Baig shared that phone usage can create a behavioural addiction and a constant sense of obligation, leading to unintended stress.[12]

And because this stress feels unpleasant, the body's natural response then is to want to check the phone to make that stress goes away. But while doing so might calm you down for the short term, in the long run it only makes things worse. Anytime you check your phone, you are likely to find something else stressful waiting for you—another news item, an upsetting social media comment, etc.—leading to another spike in cortisol and another craving to check your phone to make your anxiety go away. This cycle, when continuously reinforced, leads to chronically elevated cortisol levels thereby contributing to burnout and related health issues.

Given that phones are notorious for taking over our time and stressing us out, the more we regulate its use, the better it is. To that end, follow these practical ideas:

- **Practice the 90:60:30 rule.** Avoid looking at your phone for the first ninety minutes after you wake up. Don't look

at it for the first sixty minutes after you return from work.
And keep it away thirty minutes before you go to bed.

- **Keep it out of sight.** When working, going for meetings
  or spending time with family and friends, leave the phone
  behind or keep it out of sight. Its mere presence, even if
  silent, as we know, is distracting. By leaving it behind or
  in another room, you will not only be able to focus better,
  but also be fully present when in the company of others.
- **Turn off notifications**. The silence will give you the quiet
  time you need.
- **Go grey**. Colourful icons are appealing and tempting;
  they reward our brain every time we unlock the phone. Set
  your phone to greyscale to eliminate those temptations.
  You will note you will check your phone less.
- **Limit your first page to just tools apps** (maps, camera,
  calendar, notes, etc.). Move the rest of your apps, especially
  mindless ones, off the first page and into folders. When you
  don't see them staring at your face, you won't miss them.
- **Remove social media**. This one can be hard but worth
  the effort. It's the easiest way to reclaim time and focus.
- **Check your phone at designated hours**. To avoid giving
  in to your impulses, allocate specific times when you will
  look at your phone. It requires willpower and discipline,
  to say the least.
- **Leave it outside the bedroom.** Avoid using it for your
  wake-up alarm. Buy an alarm clock for your bedside. Not
  only will this small change allow you to sleep well, it will
  also give you peaceful moments as you wake up in the
  morning.

Take time off

Just as taking a twenty-minute break can be refreshing, vacations too can offer a similar benefit.

Research shows that leisure and free time can lower stress and build positive moods. They can make you more creative, productive, promotable and happier as well. And what's great is that these effects linger for some time, post vacation. Jessica Bloom and colleagues from the Netherlands and Germany found that a vacation of fourteen days generated an improvement in health and well-being.[13] It peaked on the eighth vacation day and rapidly returned to baseline levels within the first week of resuming work.

A survey by Korn Ferry, a leadership and talent consulting firm, found improvements in sleep quality, moods, and blood pressure at the end of a vacation. Around 64 per cent of people shared that they were refreshed and excited to get back to work after a vacation.[14]

That levels of stress go down after a vacation was noted by Dalia Etzion from Tel Aviv University.[15] She compared a group of workers who took their annual vacation to those who did not go for a vacation during the same period. Results showed that after returning from the break, stress and burnout decreased among the vacation group compared to the non-vacation group.

Vacations can also boost creativity purely because of the different experiences we are exposed to. David Strayer, professor at the University of Utah, and his colleagues showed that hiking outdoors, disconnected from all devices for four days, led to a 50 per cent spike in creativity.[16] According to Sabine Sonnentag of the University of Mannheim in Germany, disengaging from work during time off makes you resilient in the face of stress, and more productive and engaged at work.[17]

What is critical about vacations is the detachment part. No benefits are accrued if you do the same things that you do at work. Sonnentag suggests that gaining emotional distance from highly demanding work helps people recover faster from stress. When you detach or divert your mind away from work, the body gets a chance to rebuild its expended resources. By engaging in light and diverse activities, as usually done during a vacation, you don't spend intense amounts of energy. You, in fact, save and create more for future use. Contrastingly, if all you do is think about and/or do work during your time off, it doesn't help. It only aggravates your stress levels. In that case, you are better off not taking any time off!

Several leaders vouch for this experience. For my ex-boss Kevin, his annual deer-hunting vacation served as therapy. 'It not only gives me the much-needed rest, but also energizes me to the nth limit. I come back recharged.' For Sonia, a manager at a manufacturing company who has shielded herself from burnout, 'Vacations are like vitamins. You've got to take them regularly to stay healthy.'

To wash off your stress and prevent burnout, take time off. Leave aside the worry that your commitment and career advancement will be jeopardized if you go on vacations. In fact, research by Project: Time Off indicated the opposite.[18] It showed that workers who took eleven or more vacation days were more likely to have received a raise or a bonus in the previous three years than workers who took ten or fewer days off. Only 23 per cent of those who forfeited their days were promoted in 2017, compared to 27 per cent of 'non-forfeiters'. The researchers attributed this to the fact that people who take vacations are likely to be more refreshed, relaxed and resilient through the year.

To be diligent about taking vacations, do the following:

- **Calendar your vacation time for the entire year, upfront.** Mark a copy to your boss and team.
- **Plan it right.** Schedule your time off right after concluding a stress-intensive project, or align it with school holidays or long weekends. Whether it is Labour Day, Diwali or Christmas, it is easier to extend a three-day holiday weekend to a five-day vacation week.
- **Detach.** Disconnect from your emails and meetings during vacations. That's the secret of reaping the true benefits of time off.

Reflection Points

1. As the third level of the Well-being State Pyramid, mental focus is about doing things effectively and efficiently. Introducing efficiencies at work and home can lower stress and beat burnout.

2. The ten pillars of 'work smart', writing the to-do list, working in accordance to your energy levels, leveraging the calendar tool, staying out of the inbox, running effective meetings, saying no, delegating or outsourcing, controlling phone usage, and taking breaks and time off, make robust interventions to enhance well-being.

Understand the need or 'why' to change

What needs to change?

How to change?

Focus on the process, not the outcome

Create rituals to abide by the process

Change one thing at a time

Understand the need for consistency and
perseverance

It can take two to four months to form
a new habit

18

Change Management: Consistent Actions Lead to Change

IT WAS IN 2009 that I bought my first ever BlackBerry. Just the thought of it was exciting and exhilarating. 'I am going to have the whole world at my fingertips. I can connect with anyone I want to, get more work done, free up my time.' And so on and so forth. I had the entire business case primed in my head to justify this expensive purchase.

And from there on, I was unstoppable: responding to emails left, right and centre, drafting communications on the go, or calling people the instant I thought of them. I was wired at all times. So much so that I acquired a reputation of working 24x7. If I didn't respond to emails within five minutes, I would get a call for a follow-up response, and at times out of concern to check I was doing okay.

This was just one of my quirks that began to tell on my health and well-being. A couple of years later, I ended up in hospital for exhaustion and unexplained abdominal pains.

The simplest ever advice for all the pain I went through was 'slow down and take it easy'.

Really? And easier said than done, right?

Perhaps this is what you are thinking after going through the many pages to this point. Making a change is hard. So much so that even thinking about it can be overwhelming. You may also be concerned about finding the time and energy to do this now. Alternatively, you may have the inclination and resources, but you don't know exactly how to go about it.

- Where do I start?
- How do I change?
- What would it take?

A structured approach to change

As a change expert for my organization, you would think I knew all about enabling change. I did. Theoretically, to make others change. I had all the right tools and tactics. But to transpose that learning to myself was tough. I had to work hard to 'slow down and take it easy'.

To enable a change of any magnitude, you have to first understand the 'burning platform': the reason or 'why' you want to change. If your reason is convincing enough to you, you will go all the way to make that happen. If you truly believe you are not in a happy space—burned out or nearing burnout, or that your relationships are at stake—that's a strong enough impetus for change. Once that 'why' is bold and clear, the next steps become relatively easier.

The second step is to identify the change: what you want to change. This, of course, involves knowing your current state. What are the pain points and dials you need to tweak to get to your desired state? Recall, we did this exercise early on to identify our priorities. Knowing where you are, where you want to be, and how you intend to bridge the gaps between the two make the crux of planning the change.

For my personal challenge of curtailing BlackBerry usage, I literally went through each of the 'change' steps first in my mind and then wrote them out on a sheet of paper. This exercise clarified several things that I had taken for granted or glossed over.

1. To get off my BlackBerry, I had to understand why I wanted to do so: my health was at stake. It was far more important than feeding my exhilarating drive or seeking that next promotion.
2. Recognizing my 'burning platform', I then undertook the current and desired state exercise. In the current state, I was on the phone constantly. In my desired state, I wanted to limit my usage to specific hours. I wanted to set boundaries.
3. To achieve my desired state, I decided to tweak the process, not the outcome. Let me explain this.

Focus on the process, not the outcome

One of the upsides of change management, or any continuous improvement methodology, is that it asks you to focus on the inputs and the process, not on the outcome. When your inputs are right, and you give them the right mix, your results will be right too. Take the basic example of preparing a dish. We focus on the ingredients and the recipe—the inputs and the art of mixing them up—and, boom, the result is what you expected. Note, you didn't focus on the finished product at the beginning. You focused on the process.

So where am I going with this? You see, to enable a personal change, we need to focus on the process, not the results.

Several researchers have looked at this from an empirical standpoint. One that comes to mind is psychologist Carol Dweck who has conducted experiments with thousands of kids to help them blossom to their full potential.[1] Dweck talked about focusing on the 'process of praise' to foster a growth mindset that would in turn yield positive outcomes. She emphasized that we need to praise the process that kids engage in: their effort, their strategies or their focus, their perseverance, instead of praising their intelligence, talent or grades. When you praise the effort, you remove their obsession of focusing solely on the end result, which has the potential to overwhelm them. By praising them at every step, you build their belief in themselves, which gets them closer to their goal of delivering a remarkable performance.

Not surprisingly, in her study, students who were not praised for this growth mindset continued to show declining grades, but those who were praised for their effort showed a sharp rebound in their grades.

The same logic applies to us adults. To initiate a change, focus on the inputs and the process of doing it right, not the outcome.

In my case, I altered the process to keep my BlackBerry out of sight and look at it only at predefined times. To follow and adhere to this process, I created a ritual around it.

Create rituals

Rituals comprise of a series of steps that are practised in a specific order (top to bottom), repeatedly and consistently. They offer a structure to go about our activities. For example, for most of us, a morning ritual is to wake up in the morning, get off the bed, go to the bathroom, brush our teeth, go to the kitchen, make coffee, and so on. They are little steps that we follow without even being aware that we are doing them. Of course, we arrived at this stage by practising them in the same way, at the same time, every single day.

To enable a change and to sustain it, rituals come in handy.

For my BlackBerry challenge, I altered my environment by creating the following ritual:

- Turn off the phone when I reach work.
- Put it away in my handbag.
- Stash the handbag in my office closet.
- Finish two items on the to-do list.
- Take out the phone.
- Look at messages/emails for twenty minutes.
- Put the phone back in the closet.
- Take it out only after the next round of work gets done.

By engaging in these steps every single day, I formed a new habit of handling my BlackBerry.

Similarly, to start exercising regularly, instead of focusing on developing the habit of 'working out', consider the following ritual:

- Wake up in the morning.
- Brush your teeth.
- Change into your workout clothes.
- Fill up your water bottle.
- Head to the gym.
- Turn on the exercise machine.

These rituals, on repeated use, become habits.

Now, to prime for action and internalize rituals, create visual cues. For instance, you can print these steps on a sticky note and put them up in a place where you can see them easily. Perhaps the best place would be the bathroom mirror. As you wake up and go to wash your face, the sticky note would remind you of the next step: 'Change into your workout clothes.'

Alternatively, the night before, keep your shoes and other gear in your line of sight next to your bed. The mere sight of them in the morning will remind you to associate those cues with what you have to do next.

After a while, you'll start to notice that when you wake up, you automatically throw on your workout clothes and head to the gym. You get so used to this that you even start to look forward to it, and maybe even feel that something in your life is off when you don't work out. Your ritual has now become a habit. It has become seamlessly integrated into your daily routine.

And as you succeed, that will continue to reinforce and motivate you further. Isn't this process of rituals about being mindful too? Only when you are aware and fully present can you become personally involved in the process and note its value.

By building and integrating small rituals into your routine and engaging in them repeatedly for two to four months, new habits can be formed.

Take baby steps

To initiate any change, take baby steps. Go slow to avoid getting overwhelmed. Most of our change efforts fail because we take on too many drastic changes at a time. Our willpower begins to wane when we take on too much.

In 1998, Roy Baumeister and colleagues from Case Western Reserve University found that those who were forced to exert willpower—resisting cookies placed in front of them—did worse on puzzles and problem-solving tasks than people who indulged.[2] This was attributed to the fact that the group that exercised self-control had used up all their fuel and had no more left for problem solving. They called this phenomenon 'ego depletion'. This is why after a hard day's work all you want is to hit the couch and do nothing. You have depleted all your resources. Similar is the case when you take on too many or too difficult tasks. You experience ego depletion.

To avoid this, it is best to change one habit at a time.

How you perceive the task also matters, whether it is daunting or easy. For example, if you want to jump on to the fitness wagon and decide you want to work out for ninety minutes per day six days per week, that is going to feel like a daunting task. Because it feels gigantic, you're far more likely to give it up. Whereas if you decide to walk for ten minutes after dinner each night, that feels fairly easy to accomplish, and therefore it is.

The beautiful thing is that once you've adopted the 'easy mode' version of your desired task, you can always amp it up afterwards. For example, if you walk for ten minutes after dinner each night for a month, it won't sound so difficult when you say, 'Hey, I'll walk for twenty-five minutes now.' Then you can try out a bit of running. And before you know it, you may be working out thirty minutes per day, six days per week.

Take help and monitor your progress

To ensure you practise your rituals and keep your commitment to change, leverage the help of someone you are close to: your spouse, colleague or friend who can hold you accountable. Having that support can quicken the process of habit creation. Also keep a log of your progress. For instance, to track your exercise regimen, keep a diary to record your daily effort: what you did, for how long, how many calories were burned. Visual progress, or lack thereof, can keep you in check.

Reflection Points
1. Know the 'why' or reason to change.
2. Identify the root cause or what needs to change.
3. Delineate steps to enable the change.
4. Create rituals and make them visible.
5. Be consistent and persevere. It takes two to four months to develop a new habit.

PART III

Environmental Strategies to Beat Burnout

A positive environment can make all the difference to our well-being

Organizations and societies, through humane cultures and supportive work policies and regulations, can prevent the onset of burnout

19

Create Humane Organizations
and Societies

Have you heard the story about the rescue of a drowning person from a rushing river?

Here's how it goes:

A bystander sees someone drowning in the river. He quickly jumps in and saves that person. He is just about to go his own way when he spots another struggling person and pulls him out as well. After a half-dozen repetitions, the rescuer suddenly starts to run along the bank even as the river sweeps yet another floundering person into view. 'Aren't you going to rescue that fellow?' asks another bystander. 'Heck no,' the rescuer replies. 'I am going upstream to find out what's pushing all these people in in the first place.'

By fixing the upstream, the bystander wanted to prevent downstream drowning.

Burnout too requires an upstream fix—altering the environment that triggers it in the first place.

Thus far, we have focused primarily on the downstream, strengthening the individual. Let's turn our attention now to the upstream: what organizations and societies can do together to guard us against burnout.

Humane organizations

The 'all employee meeting' filled us with trepidation. The leader in no ambiguous terms set the tone. His words were ringing in my ears. 'If you don't deliver, there will be a bloodbath. You will lose your jobs. And you don't want that, do you? I want each of you to get to work and hit those targets with full focus and precision. I want to hear the cash register ring in money this quarter, unlike the previous one.'

There was a strange silence in the room. We all looked at each other as if each of us had just been singled out for not delivering. It was an unpleasant feeling. To use severe words that threaten and disparage can only instil fear rather than draw motivation or engagement from anyone at all.

We quietly left the meeting, feeling insecure and low.

On the other side of the fence was our divisional leader who conveyed the message differently. He said, 'I know we didn't hit the targets this time, but we can make up for that. We are all in this together. Let's go at it with all our might. My team and I are here to work with you.' He was inspiring, motivating and believed in bringing people along versus threatening them into delivering results. His leadership set a different tone, embodying a humane approach.

When the culture is humane and caring, employees feel safe, motivated and driven to give their discretionary effort.

But when it is brutal or authoritarian, and devoid of care or sensitivity, it is only replete with stress, anxiety and toxicity.

To prevent or stop burnout downstream, we need a conducive climate upstream. We need humane organizations. Where targets are important, but so are employee respect and health. Where the 'what' matters, but so does the 'how'. This does not imply that one has to be 'soft' or 'too nice'; one can still lead powerfully, exert authority and influence, communicate with empathy, and show concern and consideration towards others. This approach aligns with psychologist Carl Rogers's view according to which, to achieve their full potential, people need a growth-promoting environment that is characterized by acceptance, genuineness and empathy,[1] an environment that enhances theirs and the organization's well-being and performance.

Research by Professor Kim Cameron at the University of Michigan showed that workplaces characterized by caring, supportive, respectful, honest and forgiving relationships demonstrated better organizational results.[2] Likewise, Jane Dutton, also at the University of Michigan and co-author of *Awakening Compassion at Work*, highlighted that compassion can foster greater workplace resilience.[3]

Researchers Sigal Barsade and Olivia O'Neill at Wharton and George Mason University, respectively, talk about the culture of companionate love, where colleagues take care of each other.[4] They found that when employees ask and care about each other's work and non-work issues, they are more engaged. They are careful of each other's feelings, show compassion when things don't go well, and also show affection and caring—and that can be by bringing somebody a cup of coffee when you go get your own, or just listening when a co-worker needs to talk.' Most importantly, people who feel free to express affection for one another are more committed to the organization, satisfied with their jobs, and accountable for their performance.

Clearly, 'soft' gestures can significantly drive engagement and impact organizational results.

Why wouldn't we want such organizations that benefit employees personally and professionally?

Start with a committed leadership

For any transformation, the onus rests on the top branch: the CEO. One who willingly and with conviction treats this 'soft' philosophy as a business imperative, defining the business case and mobilizing the organization towards achieving a humane culture. Who recognizes why it is important and what the organization is missing by not having it as mainstream today.

A committed leadership then sets the tone, walks the talk, communicates and reinforces the importance of such culture by allocating resources and choosing their trusted leaders to spearhead this change. As that happens, the strategy is defined, the dials to tweak are communicated, the metrics are established, and the behaviours they wish to reinforce are modelled. With committed leadership, the organization gets aligned to this new vision.

Take, for example, the case of Aetna, the insurance company. With CEO Mark Bertolini's vision, the company launched its holistic wellness programme for its entire employee base. Similarly, because of active support from the leadership, Johnson & Johnson floated their vision on well-being a few years ago. The fruits of their work transformed into an anti-burnout programme that they launched in March 2017. Costing more than $1,00,000 per leader, it obviously had the support and backing of the executive leadership.

Can you imagine something of this magnitude without the CEO's support?

Implement conducive policies and practices

To back and sustain a humane culture, there need to be relevant policies and practices in place. For these are the very elements that support and nudge the work culture in the desired direction.

Consider this example that LeAnne, a senior HR leader at a large global organization in Illinois, shared with me.

'I still recall, it was a very different kind of workday for us. The vibes were different. Employees who are normally rushing around from one meeting to another were walking hand in hand with their children. The whole workplace had a light and calming kind of a feel. Smiles and positive interactions were visible across the hallways. I found myself smiling as I walked down to get my lunch. My heart felt warm. It was "Bring your child to work day".'

It is amazing how that simple initiative changed the mood of the organization, she said. 'It was a reminder that we are humans after all, not robotic machines. To see the company and your colleagues supporting you in what's so important to you—your kids and your family—was extremely encouraging. Just to feel connected with something so basic and beautiful, we should be doing similar activities once a quarter or so.'

Such practices not only improve the mood of the organization on that particular day, they also drive employee engagement and loyalty for the longer term. 'When you feel cared for or believe the organization is supportive of you, you give more of our discretionary effort then,' said LeAnne.

Flexible work arrangements, which offer control over your work hours or schedule, is another means to promoting employee well-being. Linda Thomas from Bellevue University and Daniel Ganster from the University of Arkansas found that flexible scheduling along with supervisor support positively influenced employee perceptions of control over their work and family matters.[5] Employees perceived less work–family conflict, job dissatisfaction, depression and health complaints.

Clearly, small changes of this kind can have long-lasting impacts on personal health, relationships, engagement, performance and bottom lines.

Watch out for the time drainers

Apart from putting in new practices, it is equally vital to revisit those that are time or energy drainers. Typical ones include too many meetings and a hyperactive email culture. Controlling such extremes can lower stress levels and enhance productivity for all concerned.

A very senior leader, Anne, who had global responsibility for one of her company's businesses, shared what she referred to as the 'five meetings' protocol. Her boss was infamous for driving unnecessary amounts of work for his direct reports.

She shared the following:

'To prepare for my boss' meeting, my leadership team would first get together. That was Meeting 1. Meeting 2 was to present to me what we planned to present to my boss. Meeting 3 was the dry run. Meeting 4 was the actual meeting with my boss and peers. Meeting 5 was a debrief with my team: things the boss wanted differently or in addition.

'By the time we were done with this close-to-a-month-long preparation, it was time for the next month's meeting. And the cycle would begin again. There was no time for any actual work, and worse, these meetings didn't yield any productive outcomes. They were a complete waste of time. Imagine the amount of time and grief we could have avoided if this review was done differently or under less pressure.'

Too many emails and the expectation of an immediate response are also known to augment stress levels. Of course, this stress can be reduced by individuals managing their inbox smartly, but organizations too can set the tone in this regard. One option is to stall emails, especially during non-work hours so employees can truly disconnect from work. Several companies have taken a lead in this direction. Volkswagen deactivated employees' mobile email accounts after work hours. No emails were forwarded to company mobile phones between 6 p.m. and 7 a.m.[6] Allianz, another German company, told employees that they didn't have to answer emails on weekends or during vacation time. Daimler went a step further, automatically deleting emails that are sent while someone was on vacation. Instead of the usual out of office message, contacts got a notification that their email hadn't gone through, and they could either try to reach an alternate person or try again when the vacationer was back.[7]

When organizations take such stands, it is easier for employees to disconnect without any guilt or fear of repercussions.

Develop humane leaders

'Nero played the fiddle while Rome burned.'

According to popular belief, Nero, the Roman emperor, preferred to play music rather than comfort his people when Rome was burning. He was rumoured to be a self-centred, inattentive and irresponsible leader.

Humane leaders aren't like Nero. Far from it, they are down in the trenches with their people. Their job is to be in the right place and pay attention to the right things. They care, they engage, and they create benefits for their employees and organizations.

Research shows that the most powerful way leaders can improve employee well-being is not just through programmes and initiatives, but through their daily interactions with employees. A large study by Anna Nyberg and colleagues at the Karolinska Institute showed that while having a harsh boss is linked to heart problems in employees, inspiring, empathic and supportive bosses are associated with loyal and engaged employees.[8]

Similarly, the Energy Project study showed that feeling cared for by one's supervisor has a more significant impact on people's sense of trust and safety than any other behaviour demonstrated by a leader.[9] Employees who claim they have more supportive supervisors are 1.3 times as likely to stay with the company and are 67 per cent more engaged. Psychologist

Michelangelo Vianello from the University of Padua in Italy found that when leaders were polite, respectful, sensitive or willing to make sacrifices for their teams, their employees felt more loyal and committed towards them.[10]

As Ganesh, CEO at Etnyre International, said: 'You don't have to coddle your employees, but just be there for them. Listen to them and guide them. Instead of saying, "You are in trouble" or "You are screwed", tell them "We will get through this", "You are doing a fine job" or "We are in it together." These are the words that would motivate them to rise above and beyond.'

By reinforcing such leader behaviours, organizations can promote a culture of emotional safety and engagement. Training leaders to show concern, understanding and empathy towards others can make all the difference. What's more, Nicholas Christakis from the department of social and natural science at Yale University and James Fowler at the University of California, San Diego, the authors of *Connected*, suggest that these behaviours are contagious. If you're kind, those around you will also act kindly. It spreads around you, multiplying its benefits.[11]

Again, being a humane leader doesn't mean you forget about the results. What it does mean is that you drive results, but with a humane and personal touch.

Monitor employee workloads

Tracking employee workload can also help prevent burnout.

Boston Consulting Group flags employees working too many long weeks with what is called a 'red zone report'. When a consultant clocks more than sixty hours per week over five weeks, he or she is flagged on reports that are reviewed by their seniors. If the episode continues, a Career Development Committee sponsor is charged with finding ways to bring the hours down either by advising the employee on time management, extending the project timeline, taking some load off, or adding more resources.[12]

Such processes can enable an even distribution of workload and keep an eye on those who may be feeling the brunt of consistent overwork.

Create networking avenues

Relationships with co-workers can lower stress, promote job satisfaction and beat burnout. To foster a sense of belonging at work, networking platforms can come to the rescue. Happy hours, hobby clubs, team activities and other means make good avenues for employees to interact and connect with each other. Actively matching employees with potential mentors and coaches can also serve a similar purpose. Such forums would not only promote employee development and establish connections, but also offer them the necessary support structure that could be leveraged as needed.

Implement training programmes

A team of researchers conducted a study to assess how training programmes on schedule control and supervisory support for personal life may help employees manage their work–family challenges.[13] Erin Kelly of the Department of Sociology and Minnesota Population Center, University of Minnesota, and colleagues found that employees who participated in the intervention showed greater decreases in their work–family conflict and greater increases in health behaviours such as sleep hours. They concluded that deliberate organizational interventions can positively influence employees' work–family situations.

What's more, such practices can also have a far-reaching positive impact on their families. A study by Susan McHale from Pennsylvania State University and team noted that for employees who attended 75 per cent or more training sessions on 'schedule control and support', their adolescent children reported more time with their parents, greater parental involvement in their studies, and overall more interactions, compared to those whose parents attended less than 75 per cent of the sessions.[14]

As mentioned above, developing leaders in these areas is as critical. They need to be made aware of the implications of their extreme expectations along with the value of their support for employee productivity and well-being. Relevant learning and tools need to be made accessible so they can be effective in identifying at-risk cases of burnout within their teams.

Introduce holistic well-being programmes

Beyond the traditional employee assistance programmes, consider other ways to augment employee health and well-being. Offerings such as yoga, meditation, along with awareness sessions on healthy eating, sleeping and exercising for good health, performance and well-being, can be highly effective.

As I mentioned earlier, the health insurance giant Aetna implemented a holistic programme for its entire employee base. Likewise, Johnson & Johnson floated an anti-burnout programme for its top executives and a lighter version of it for the rest of the employees. Other leading companies like Procter & Gamble and Goldman Sachs Group offer free courses on sleep hygiene to highlight the importance of optimal rest. Similarly, Google and Nike improved their company's sleep culture by incorporating a flexible approach to work schedules and providing nap pods in their offices.

Reinforce by consistent communication

Communication is key to this transformation. Talk about the culture you are trying to create. Leverage different portals internally and externally to showcase your success stories, the behaviours you are reinforcing and how the organization is benefiting because of this shift towards a humane culture. Spotlight and recognize leaders who walk the talk. Communicate similar messages externally as well. Position the organization as a great place to work, one that believes in employee well-being through humane actions and behaviours.

Humane societies

When close to 50 per cent of the population is burned out—exhausted, indifferent and in some extreme cases harbouring suicidal thoughts—there is obviously something very wrong with this picture. It would be incorrect to assume that all of them are ill-equipped or have personal deficits of some sort to tackle situations.

Beyond the organizations, the root cause of burnout resides in our societal expectations. Very early on, through socialization at home and outside, we learn the value of hard work, and what success is and isn't. It is this same culture that also reinforces the importance of perfect grades, great jobs, promotions and wealth. All without talking about the price of burnout that we pay to achieve this kind of success.

To shift the focus towards well-being, society needs to redefine success. A definition that goes beyond the traditional material markers to one characterized by shared values of happiness, contentment, and prioritized by care and growth for self and others.

But the bigger question is, where does one begin this change and how?

Undoubtedly, a change of this order requires a 'systems' approach where interdisciplinary stakeholders come together to pool their minds and resources to achieve this common vision. The government in partnership with policymakers and progressive thinkers can pool their focus by implementing practices that facilitate individual well-being.

Standardize work hours and practices
Given the fact that overwork and unlimited work hours are significant determinants of burnout, one of the plausible solutions is to mandate standardized work hours and related practices.

The government can lawfully reinstate the traditional 8 a.m. to 5 p.m. work hours keeping in mind the overarching health of the society. In some parts of the world, this change has already begun. In 2017, France instituted a labour law called the 'Right to Disconnect'.[15] Similar rulings are being enacted in Italy, Philippines, Germany and Luxembourg.[16] Recently, South Korea came up with a legislation limiting weekly work hours to fifty-two from its maximum of sixty-eight.[17] New York City too is looking to stop emails after office hours. Similar to the French law, this bill would make it unlawful for employees to check and respond to emails and other electronic communications during non-work hours.[18]

Some countries have initiated compressed work weeks. Perpetual Guardian, a New Zealand company that manages trusts and estates, trialled a four-day work week. They found it to be a success, with gains in job satisfaction, collaboration, efficiency and productivity.[19] Likewise, a twenty-three-month study in Gothenburg, Sweden's second-largest city, looked at the effects that a reduced workday had on the productivity of sixty-eight full-time nurses. What they found was that the nurses were happier, healthier and more energetic when they worked six-hour days instead of eight.[20]

An effective practice can be to compensate employees for the work they put in beyond the standard work hours. The threat of a significant cash drain would likely bring organizations to better control their work hours and expectations. In parallel, the government can consider implementing especially designed tax credit schemes to nudge organizations in this direction. For example, workplaces that do curtail work hours, meet 'standards', live by 'humane practices' or compensate employees for overtime can benefit from especially designed governmental schemes.

Ban technology that erodes societies
We all are aware that technology brings a mixed bag of outcomes. Researchers Paul Best, Roger Manktelow and Brian Taylor from the UK have shown that social media platforms come

with intentionally designed negatives that cause interference with the human mind.[21] There is depression, isolation, fear of missing out, and a lot more, leading to significant healthcare costs and concerns for the society as a whole.

But despite these known negatives, we are unable to control their proliferation. Though the usage of technology is an individual decision, it is also a fact that we are vulnerable to temptation. Legal regulations can come to our aid to help us control our impulses. To that end, mechanisms can be put in place to sanction products that protect human minds rather than impair them. Take, for example, social media companies that generate revenue by tempting us to stay glued on their platforms. Considering the negative impact of these deliberate tactics, the government can challenge them and others to come up with different business models instead. Accordingly, businesses can be asked to incorporate the negative impacts of their products on the human psyche. Just as emissions or carbon footprints are monitored, a similar focus can be allotted to this issue as well.

Start early
Instead of trying to beat burnout in adult life, its onset can be stalled early on.

Practices that we are encouraging organizations and professionals to adopt can begin in schools. Whether it is making the performance assessment and the learning process less stressful, introducing mindfulness, training on time management skills, or teaching adequate coping skills, the right blend can be integrated into school curriculums.

Some winds of change are already noticeable in this space. Finland is reinforcing that learning matters more than education. Instead of control, competition and standardized testing, the schools are concentrating more on warmth, collaboration and teacher-led encouragement and assessment. Scholar and author Pasi Sahlberg in his book *Finnish Lessons* emphasises teacher and leader professionalism, building trust between the society and its schools, and investing in educational equity rather than in competition.[22]

In a major move to reduce emphasis on grades, the Singapore Ministry of Education is doing away with examinations and graded assessments for Primary 1 and 2 students from 2019. It has a phased approach to take this further to other grades. This move aims to free up more time in schools to strengthen students' holistic development, self-discovery and engaged learning. In parallel, the report cards will be refreshed with a holistic developmental profile. Under the revised criteria, students will be assessed on attributes of diligence, curiosity, collaboration and enthusiasm in daily lessons and learning activities. Similar to Finland, their motto is that learning shouldn't be an act of competition.[23]

Some universities too have adopted similar evaluation practices. For example, as freshmen at the Massachusetts Institute of Technology, students receive grades of Pass or No Record. A grade of C or better equals Pass, noted as P on their transcripts. Non-passing grades of D or F only show up on internal transcripts. The goal is to encourage students to learn and collaborate without worrying about grade performance.[24]

Apart from these, school curriculums can integrate activities to build students' physical, emotional and mental capabilities. An active focus on exercise, healthy eating, sleeping, taking breaks or engaging in extracurricular activities or mindfulness can give children a good head start towards addressing their well-being. In line with this, in India, the education minister of Delhi, Manish Sisodia, introduced mindfulness classes in government schools.[25] Professor Mark Greenberg from Pennsylvania University reinforces the fact that mindfulness is a feasible and effective method for building resilience among students.[26] It facilitates improved student learning and supports their psychological, physiological and social development.

We would be well on our way to becoming a humane society if:

Forbes showcases the top fifty most 'content' people rather than the richest.

Schools communicate student well-being indices along with academic feats.

The financial scorecards of organizations are inclusive of their positive impact on the society.

Individuals measure their affluence by well-being instead of wealth alone.

Reflection Points

1. Humane organizations and societies are critical partners in the well-being equation.
2. An organizational growth work culture is far more conducive to well-being than one focused on financial success alone.
3. Through legislation, the government can take an active stand in mitigating burnout at a societal level.

PART IV

Burnout among Children

Burnout among children is common

Parents, teachers, schools and
children can come together to prevent it

20

Prepare Your Children to Thrive in a Dog-eat-dog World

It was in 2017 when I first learned about Sonya, a student in an international school in Thailand. She was recovering from burnout then. Her challenge started in grade 11, and continued through her graduating years in school.

Sonya was a high achiever and until grade 10 at the top of her class. Just like many others, she too was aiming for admission to a reputed college in the US.

Her mother said, 'Like other kids, Sonya had quite a lot on her plate. She was stressed about her grades. But at what point that stress transformed into burnout, we have no idea. We could tell things were not right when she started getting anxiety attacks and developed a phobia of school. She started to miss school and her grades began to slide rather quickly. She would cry and stay locked in her room. We eventually took her to a psychologist who informed us she was burned out.'

Sonya's case isn't an isolated one. Pressures of academic excellence are very much pervasive in students' lives. According to the American Psychological Association, stress and burnout are top health concerns for US teens between grades 9 and 12.[1] Dr Jeff Devens, from the Singapore American School, said: 'At any given time, you have six to a dozen high-schoolers showing signs of depression, anxiety, burnout, self-injury or suicidal ideation. There may be another twenty or so who are thinking along these lines, ideating but not acting. There are myriad reasons as to why; academic performance is certainly one of them. For example, some students who get straight As until grade 11 are unable to handle the anxiety and emotional pain when they earn a B grade. They conclude that they are not smart enough, that their chances of getting into top colleges are grim. Not knowing how to cope, some employ unhealthy means to address the hurt.'

The prevalence of student burnout mirrors adult burnout. It is universal and has common symptoms. A study by Rebecca Ang and Vivien Huan from Nanyang Technological University, Singapore, showed that the more academic stress there is, the more the likelihood of burnout.[2] Too many school activities, feelings of inadequacy, lack of interest and pressure to meet family expectations are also likely contributors to burnout, suggests a Turkish study led by researcher Ayse Aypay.[3]

Similar results were noted among other young adult populations. Wilmar Schaufeli, Marisa Salanova, Vicente González-romá and Arnold Bakker from Utrecht University, the Netherlands, studied a group of undergraduate students from Spain, Portugal and the Netherlands.[4] They found that burnout was prevalent in all countries and inversely correlated to university engagement and performance. The more burned out they were, the poorer they fared in engagement and other outcomes.

The incidence of burnout is significantly high among the medical student fraternity as well. It begins in medical school, continues through the residency period, and finally matures in the daily life of practising physicians. The incidence of burnout ranges between 31 and 50 per cent among students and gradually rises to 50 and 76 per cent during the residency period. In fact, it has been found that 28 per cent of residents experience a major depressive episode during their training in contrast to 7–8 per cent of similarly aged individuals in the US general population.[5]

Aside from self-imposed pressures, parents too play an active role in fuelling burnout. 'When parents are highly ambitious, they tend to expect the same from their children. We see this commonly here in Singapore, a place that's full of Type A go-getter kind of professionals. They are pushing their kids hard. If I say the child isn't ready or should not take a heavy load in grade 11, they challenge me and insist their child takes on that burden. When that happens, children get overwhelmed, anxious and fear the worst. Those who cannot take this pressure succumb to burnout,' shared a teacher at the Singapore American School.

Living in burned-out homes can also do damage. It is here that children observe and emulate their parents. They learn that it's okay to sacrifice their life to achieve success, that it's fine to not take breaks or spend time with the family, and that it is okay to work non-stop at the expense of their well-being. Though these children may turn out to be as hardworking and dedicated as their parents, they are also already predisposed to burnout. A study led by the Academy of Finland[6] found that burnout experiences were shared in families, particularly between adolescents and parents of the same gender, that is, between daughters and mothers and between sons and fathers.

Regardless of the source, burnout comes with a significant cost to children and those around them.

The cost of child burnout

The consequences of child burnout are many. The health, mental state, relationships and academic performance of children are compromised. Efficacy and confidence decline. They become less engaged, value school less and fare poorly in academic achievement. To cope with these, they may turn to substance abuse, smoking and other negative vices; some may even harbour suicidal thoughts.

Cindy Liu, a psychologist at Brigham and Women's Hospital, found that one in five college students think about killing themselves, and some even attempt it.[7] Among more than 67,000 students surveyed, over 20 per cent said they experienced stressful events in the last year that were strongly associated with mental health problems, including harming themselves and suicidal attempts.

The feeling that one should drop out of school is another fallout of burnout. Liselotte Dyrbye and colleagues from the Mayo Clinic found that approximately 11 per cent of medical students seriously consider dropping out each year because of burnout.[8]

Apart from this significant impact on children and young adults, their families get affected too. The immediate parental reaction is that of worry and helplessness. Sonya's parents had this to say: 'It was a nightmare. We questioned our parenting. How could this happen to our child? We started blaming each other for her condition. We could see our family was crumbling right in front of our eyes. It was affecting our younger daughter. We were scared of her falling prey to this. The atmosphere at home was painful.'

Similar concern and worry were expressed by Anisha's mother, who I introduced you to earlier. 'We just didn't know what was happening to our daughter. We were shaken. While pursuing medicine was her choice, somewhere we felt we had failed as parents. Our entire family spirit had died. There was no motivation to eat, sleep or do anything till Anisha recovered.'

'When one person in the family is burned out—doesn't matter if it's the child or the adult—the entire family gets affected. The negativity and anxiety seep into all relationships within the family unit. Whether it is marriage or the parent–child relationship, its stability is rocked,' shared Dr Jyoti Chhabra during a conversation on children's burnout.

Mitigating child burnout

Just like adults, preventing burnout among children also requires all stakeholders—parents, teachers and schools to come together.

Parents

Spend time

The most important aspect of a parent–child relationship is spending time together. Whether it is in activities related to caring, playing, teaching or disciplining, parental involvement contributes towards nurturing the bond and enhancing children's overall development. It is here that they acquire basic coping and problem-solving skills and capacities to build future relationships and succeed in different environments.

Given this long-term impact, it is critical to spend undivided time with children. Focused time allows you to be aware of the happenings in your child's life on a daily basis and also alerts you to any lurking issues. Having family meals together, taking vacations, doing household chores, working on homework or engaging in other activities are perfect avenues to spend time together.

Research by Marla Eisenberg from the Division of Epidemiology, Minneapolis, and team[9] looked at over 4700 adolescents and found that frequent family mealtimes was connected with low substance abuse, better academic performance and fewer depressive symptoms. The reason? Mealtimes offered a channel to converse and connect with each other.

In one of our conversations, Dr Tony Avellino shared that he learned the importance of family time a little too late—only after he experienced burnout. After his recovery, he made it a point to spend quality time with his family. 'I had to be very conscious in planning my time with my children. Every Monday evening, I take my daughter out for dinner. And every Sunday morning, I am with my son at a cafe. And yes, a couple of times a month, I go out for lunch with my wife. Time with them gives me a peek into their lives. Not only am I up to speed on what's happening with them, I also get to share my learnings along the way. I have a strong bond with each of them now.'

Impart lessons of self-love. Let them know that they are precious and worthy. Only when they love themselves will they grow beyond their anxieties and fears. Heighten their confidence and self-efficacy through feedback and guidance. Have deep conversations about their aspirations, purpose and goals. Offer resources and any help they may need to perform to their full potential. Praise the process and encourage them to work hard without compromising their health and well-being. In parallel, teach them the value of smart work and living a life of strength and courage through exercise, rest and more. Having experienced life, share your insights on effectively warding off stress and managing varying priorities.

Be astute about any behavioural changes. If you notice anxiety, stress, depression or isolation, take it seriously. Get to the bottom of it. Do not make it light or ridicule their emotions. If you cannot address the issue, seek an expert opinion. But the important thing is to address it. Double your love, support and understanding during such times.

To sum up, practise an authoritative parenting style that is characterized by listening, warmth and firmness to cultivate psychological independence and growth among children. Kayla Cripps from Southern Illinois University, Carbondale, and Brett Zyromski from Ohio State University suggest that this style is linked with a range of positive health outcomes among children: higher life satisfaction and fewer physical and psychological complaints.[10]

Be a good role model
How you cope is how your children will learn to cope. Given the power of observational learning, watch your behaviour and interactions in front of and with them. Avoid complaining, whining and badmouthing your job, boss or anyone or anything else. Take care of yourself; attend to your needs and well-being. By practising self-love, you can effectively teach them the value of self-love and self-worth. Exercise patience and be fully present when in their company. When talking to them, look into their eyes rather than keeping your eyes on your screens or randomly nodding. Research by Ellen Galinsky at the Bank Street College of Education backs the importance of such responsive parenting.[11]

Adhere to a protocol of no work or meetings during dinner and family time. When at home, leave your work and work preoccupations in the office. Don't take out your frustrations on your kids or spouse. In fact, lighten your mood by spending quality interactive time with them. Play a game, listen to music, help with homework, or simply sit and talk. Create family rituals of sharing gratitude or any good deeds performed. Finally, take family vacations. They will not only offer you a much-needed break, but also give you a chance to spend quality time with the family. Engage in activities that the whole family can indulge in.

Encourage friendships and non-academic activities

Relationships are critical in developing social skills, self-esteem and independence. The greater the cumulative support from family and friends, the more likely it is that children will experience positive health. According to psychologist Shawn Achor, students who spend time with friends, especially when under academic pressures, are less likely to burn out.[12]

Further, being involved in different activities with others can also alleviate burnout. Sheri Jacobs, a doctoral student of psychology at the University of South Florida, and David Dodd, a senior lecturer of psychology at Washington University in St Louis, found this in a study of college students. Those involved in extracurricular activities showed fewer signs of burnout. Specifically, there was a positive relation between extracurricular activities and a sense of personal accomplishment (a dimension of burnout).[13] Extracurricular involvement, rather than leading to emotional exhaustion, promoted feelings of achievement and self-worth, thus playing a protective role against one aspect of burnout.

Clearly, a well-rounded experience leads to better health, greater happiness and success.

Monitor their screen time

Similar to adults, children too are glued to their gadgets. A recent Australian Psychology Society survey found that more than three out of four young people are highly involved with their mobile phones and are using social media on an average of 3.3 hours each day, five or more days of the week.[14] Two out of three feel the pressure to look good and nearly a third have been bullied online. Nearly half of the frequent users look at social media in bed before sleeping.

Certainly not numbers to be proud of. Not only are these time drainers, they are also energy drainers. A study by scholars Karla Murdock, Mikael Horrisian and Caroline Crichlow-Ball from Washington and Lee University, Lexington, Virginia, found that too much texting, night-time cell phone notifications, and compulsion to check them hinder sleep quality.[15]

Given the perils of technology usage, educate children about the risks and unintended consequences of Internet interactions. Discuss and, together, set boundaries for their usage. Do audits and random checks on what they are posting and talking about. As a good practice, make it a family habit to not use technology for thirty minutes to an hour before bedtime. Consider leaving devices outside the bedroom when it's time to go to sleep.

Schools and teachers

Besides the curriculum changes that we discussed in the previous chapter, more can be done by teachers and school administrators.

Create a learning environment that fosters student learning, motivation and enhances their self-efficacy. Children look for strong social ties and value acceptance, care and support from others. A Finnish study led by Katariina Salmela-Aro and colleagues shows that a negative school climate drives burnout, while support from the school and positive motivation from teachers promote well-being.[16]

Andreas Schleicher, director for education and skills at the Organisation for Economic Co-operation and Development (OECD) in Paris, found that students who reported that their teacher was willing to help and was interested in their learning were about 1.3 times more likely to feel that they belonged at school.[17] Conversely, students who reported some unfair treatment by their teachers were 1.7 times more likely to report feeling isolated at school. The importance of social support is also emphasized by others. In a meta-analysis of over 200 studies, Po Sen Chu, Donald Saucier and Eric Hafner from Kansas State University showed a positive association between social support and well-being among children and adolescents.[18] The more connected the students felt, the better they fared.

Build awareness on resilience, purpose, happiness, well-being, etc., and how these positively impact academic performance. Call it Life Lessons 101, which emphasize children's holistic development. Educate them on age-appropriate coping mechanisms so they can tackle stress effectively. Yoga, mindfulness and other practices can serve as effective tools for children to reassess their stress levels and prevent burnout.

Teach children to take charge

Principles of building physical, emotional and mental capabilities are relevant to children as well. By teaching them to be accountable for their well-being, making them aware of the perils of burnout, and equipping them with coping strategies, children can create a healthy lifestyle for themselves.

Reflection Points

1. Children and young adults are as likely to burn out as adults.
2. Quality time and open communication between parents and children can facilitate the latter's well-being.
3. Friendships and participation in extracurricular activities are as important as academics.
4. Holistic curriculums and a growth mindset culture in schools can mitigate the onset of burnout among children.

Conclusion

BOTH NATURE AND nurture chisel and define us. Given this overarching reality, burnout too is an outcome of such an interaction. To say it is solely an individual's issue or a workplace problem is simply a cop-out and forcing the monkey to stay on someone else's back. Relatedly, the remedy for beating burnout rests on both these units.

The Well-being State Pyramid offers a comprehensive framework to address burnout from an individual's standpoint. It calls for action to strengthen the individual holistically— physically, emotionally and mentally—so he or she is able to tackle daily situations with energy, coherence, clarity and, more importantly, without getting overly stressed and burned out.

To enhance your physical energy, exercise, eat right and sleep well. Science recommends working out five to seven times a week, having three balanced meals a day, and sleeping seven to nine hours a night. To bolster your emotional well-being, leverage the power of positive thinking, practise mindfulness, engage in activities that make you laugh, and spend quality time with family and friends. In addition, apply tried and tested work tactics to conclude your tasks efficiently. Writing out your to-do lists, using the calendar tool, delegating, alternating work with regular breaks, keeping the smartphone distraction away, and taking time off are some ways to reduce stress and deliver efficient results.

From an environmental vantage point, workplaces and societies play a pivotal role in facilitating individual well-being. By building humane cultures, developing humane leaders, and implementing relevant work practices, organizations can nip the onset of burnout. The onus also rests on the government and policymakers of the country who, by establishing standardized work norms and regulations, can not only help organizations manage their expectations better, but also hold them accountable for employee well-being.

Though beating burnout requires a deliberate and collaborative effort, where the individual, organization and society have to come together to achieve this common goal, the primary onus still rests on you: the individual.

Ultimately, you have the choice to prevent burnout, beat it or remain burned out.

Take the challenge and become obsessive about the well-being of you and others.

Acknowledgements

I am indebted to my colleagues, friends and the many strangers who came forward from different walks of life to share their personal stories and experiences with me. The book would have been incomplete without their candid and valuable inputs.

A sincere gratitude to Ed Rapp, who not only took the time to do the foreword for the book but also offered several insights on leading a balanced life.

Many people have helped in making the book better. I would like to especially call out Jyoti Chhabra and Sarableen Kaur for their timely inputs. Lohit Jagwani, my editor, played the devil's advocate and provided valuable suggestions on the manuscript. Thanks also to the copy-editing and other teams at Penguin Random House India.

I am extremely thankful for my family's support, particularly my parents, Vinod and R.K. Jain, my husband, Ganesh Iyer, and my daughters, Ishira and Aaina, without whom this mission would have been impossible. Thank you for giving me the space and encouragement to pursue this endeavour.

Bring It All Together:
A Sample Daily Routine

Fully recognizing that there is no one size that fits all, I am still going to share a sample daily system that includes best practices from leaders who have proactively managed to stay away from burnout. Use this protocol as a template to draft your very own and commit to practising it consistently.

The morning routine

The morning makes a critical part of the day. To channel your energies effectively, start your day right by doing the following:

1. **Get up at the same time.** Get enough sleep and develop a pattern of waking up at the same time every day.
2. **Exercise.** A workout in the morning will keep you energized through the day. Whether it is cardio, yoga or a brisk walk, pick one that you enjoy doing.
3. **No screen time.** Stay away from your phone until you are done with breakfast. Instead of getting pulled into

other people's lives on social media or emails, opt to look outside, absorb the quiet, or simply attend to your breath.

4. **Sit down for breakfast.** A healthy breakfast energizes you, improves your short-term memory, and helps you concentrate better. Allocate fifteen minutes to calmly sit down to eat.

5. **Put a smile on your face as you leave for work.** This simple act will put you in a positive frame of mind.

Getting your morning started off right is critical, but it's only half the job done. Follow a disciplined routine at work as well.

The workplace routine

1. **Write your to-do list.** Then prioritize and assign a time duration for each of your tasks. You will have better control over your time and output.

2. **Take breaks.** Performance and well-being are at their best when you alternate activity with rest. Follow the 90:20 or 52:17 rule to get the best results. And when on a break, stretch, walk or do things that relax you.

3. **Plan your meetings.** Meetings can take up all your time if you don't watch out. Attend the ones that are central to your work. Ask for the agenda and any prep material beforehand so you are effective and efficient.

4. **Respond to your emails at fixed times.** Respond to mails in batches at set times instead of attending to them the minute they hit your inbox.

5. **Single task.** Focus on your priorities one at a time so you are able to complete them versus keeping all of them in flight or as work in progress.
6. **Say no.** While showing initiative is a good thing, it comes with a cost. Carefully assess your workload and practise saying no to yourself and others.
7. **Make time for lunch.** It restores blood sugar and re-energizes you. Best to eat with colleagues than by yourself or in front of your screen.
8. **Delegate.** Leverage the power of many to free up your time. Give opportunities for others to contribute and develop.
9. **Show you care.** Recognize and thank people. Show concern. Be approachable. Be humane.

The evening routine

1. **Come home with a smile.** It will put you in a positive frame of mind.
2. **Keep the phone away.** Its mere presence can cause distraction and brain drain. Let the mind rest after a long day at work.
3. **Be present.** Have conversations with the family or attend to home chores with full attention.
4. **Eat dinner with the family.** It is good for you and the family as it keeps the communication channels open.
5. **Work after dinner if you must.** Once the chores are done and kids are busy with their homework or off to bed, conclude your work tasks.

6. **Shut down all gadgets.** Do so at least thirty minutes before hitting the bed.
7. **Wind down.** Read a book or practise five minutes of mindfulness.
8. **Gratitude.** End the night with writing three things you are grateful for. You will realize how blessed you are and that will have a calming effect on you.
9. **Be consistent.** Get to bed at a consistent time. The body becomes habituated and prepares to fall asleep at the same time.

The weekend routine

1. **Follow the same weekday routine.** Consistency keeps the cycle going.
2. **Spend time with others.** Make time for family, friends or the community. Remember to smile and laugh as you do that.
3. **Outsource.** Free yourself from transactional chores so you have time for other value-added tasks.
4. **Prepare for the week.** Assess the contents of the fridge and do other necessary prep work to ensure a smooth week ahead. Do a mental walk-though on what you are going to wear, eat and work on. This will give you a quick start with minimum energy spent on decision-making during the week.

Leverage this protocol to build your very own personal daily system.

Develop Your Personal Well-being Plan

Step 1: Are you a victim or are you accountable?

Write three concrete actions you will take to improve your accountability.

1.

2.

3.

Step 2: Find your purpose

I	Make a list of things you enjoy doing.
	1.
	2.
	3.
	4.
	5.

II	List three things people appreciate you for.			
	1.			
	2.			
	3.			

III	As a child, what did you dream of doing when you grew up?			
	1.			
	2.			
	3.			

IV	What do you dream of doing today?			
	1.			
	2.			
	3.			

V	What are the five things you will miss not accomplishing in this life or in your final moments?
	1.
	2.
	3.
	4.
	5.

VI	Identify common themes or patterns from the above.

VII	Now, write down your purpose statement in 1 to 3 sentences.

Step 3: Identify your priorities

I	Create a pie chart that identifies the major areas you spend your time in, today ('current life'). Allocate the percentage of time you spend in each area. They should total 100.
II	Create your desired pie-chart. Identify the areas where you would like to spend your time ('desired life'). Allocate percentages to those areas. They should total a 100.

III	Study the two pies and identify the areas where significant gaps exist.						
	1.						
	2.						
	3.						
	4.						
	5.						

IV	Now, list the actions you will take to get to your desired life.
	1.
	2.
	3.
	4.
	5.

Step 4: Build your energies and capabilities				
I	What will you do differently to build your physical energy?			
	1.			
	2.			
	3.			
	4.			

II	What will you do differently to enhance your emotional stability?			
	1.			
	2.			
	3.			
	4.			

III	What will you do differently to sharpen your mental focus?				
	1.				
	2.				
	3.				
	4.				

IV	Build rituals for the ones you decide to go ahead with.

Step 5: The accountability log

Start Date:

Directions: *To assess your progress, rate your satisfaction on the following items on a scale of 1 to 5, with 5 being most satisfied and 1 being the least.*

		Week 1 (1–5)	Week 2 (1–5)	Week 3 (1–5)	Week 4 (1–5)
1	I am satisfied with my physical energy levels (I eat, sleep, and exercise).				
2	I am satisfied with the way I deal with situations (I practise positive thinking, mindfulness, gratitude, spend time with family and friends, etc.).				
3	I am satisfied with the way I work (I have implemented the ten pillars of 'work smart').				
4	Overall, I am satisfied with my well-being.				

Notes:

Print this page to monitor your progress for weeks 5–8.

Notes

Introduction

1.   Future Workplace LLC and Kronos Incorporated, *Employee Engagement Lifecycle Series*, November 2016.
2.   T.D. Shanafelt, C.P. West, C. Sinsky, M. Trockel, M. Tutty, D.V. Satele and L.N. Dyrbye, 'Changes in Burnout and Satisfaction With Work–Life Integration in Physicians and the General US Working Population Between 2011 and 2017', *Mayo Clinic Proceedings* (2019).
3.   https://www.prnewswire.com/news-releases/the-nursing-skills-gap-continues-to-grow-while-70-percent-of-nurses-feel-burnt-out-in-their-current-job-according-to-new-careerbuilder-survey-300452041.html

Chapter 1: Burnout Is a Lot More Than Stress

1.   K.H. Teigen, 'Yerkes-Dodson: A Law for All Seasons', *Theory & Psychology* 4.4 (1994): 525–47.
2.   H. Selye, *The Stress of Life* (New York: McGraw-Hill, 1976).
3.   H.J. Freudenberger, 'Staff Burnout', *Journal of Social Issues* 30 (1974): 159–65.
4.   C. Maslach, 'Burned-out', *Human Behavior* 5 (1976): 16–22.
5.   http://www.katsandogz.com/onwork.html

Chapter 2: The Crisis

1. Future Workplace LLC and Kronos Incorporated, *Employee Engagement Lifecycle Series*, November 2016.
2. https://hbr.org/2017/06/burnout-at-work-isnt-just-about-exhaustion-its-also-about-loneliness
3. https://www.statista.com/statistics/418089/level-of-stress-in-us-adults-by-generation
4. https://www.gallup.com/workplace/237377/millennials-burning.aspx
5. C. Maslach, 'Burned-out', *Human Behavior* 5 (1976): 16–22.
6. T.D. Shanafelt, C.P. West, C. Sinsky, M. Trockel, M. Tutty, D.V. Satele and L.N. Dyrbye, 'Changes in Burnout and Satisfaction With Work–Life Integration in Physicians and the General US Working Population Between 2011 and 2017', *Mayo Clinic Proceedings* (2019).
7. https://www.prnewswire.com/news-releases/the-nursing-skills-gap-continues-to-grow-while-70-percent-of-nurses-feel-burnt-out-in-their-current-job-according-to-new-careerbuilder-survey-300452041.html
8. L. Lampert, 'Depression in Nurses: The Unspoken Epidemic', 2016, http://www.minoritynurse.com.
9. A. Shukla and T. Trivedi, 'Burnout in Indian Teachers', *Asia Pacific Education Review* 9.3 (2008): 320–34.
10. J. Stanley, 'How Unsustainable Workloads Are Destroying the Quality of Teaching', *Schools Week*, 13 October 2014.
11. R. Ingersoll, L. Merrill and D. Stuckey, *Seven Trends: The Transformation of the Teaching Force* (Philadelphia: Consortium for Policy Research in Education, University of Pennsylvania, 2014).
12. Liselotte N. Dyrbye, Tait D. Shanafelt, Charles M. Balch, Daniel Satele, Jeff Sloan and Julie Freischlag, 'Conflicts and Burnout among American Surgeons: A Comparison by Sex', *Archives of Surgery* 146.2 (2011): 211–17.

13. N. Beauregard, A. Marchand, J. Bilodeau, P. Durand, A. Demers and V.Y. Haines III, 'Gendered Pathways to Burnout: Results from the SALVEO Study', *Annals of Work Exposures and Health* 62.4 (2018): 426–37.

Chapter 3: Why Burnout Is Out of Control

1.   E. Stump, 'Augustine on Free Will', *The Cambridge Companion to Augustine*, 2001, pp. 124–47.
2.   L.A. Seneca, *On the Shortness of Life*, Vol. 1 (Penguin UK, 2004).
3.   L.A. Perlow and J.L. Porter, 'Making Time Off Predictable—and Required, *Harvard Business Review* 87.10 (2009): 102–09.
4.   https://blogs.wsj.com/indiarealtime/2016/05/31/indian-millennials-clock-way-more-work-hours-than-their-global-competition/
5.   https://www.ustravel.org/research/state-american-vacation-2018
6.   L. Lieke, T. van der Lippe, E.S. Kluwer and H. Flap, 'Positive and Negative Effects of Family Involvement on Work-related Burnout', *Journal of Vocational Behavior* 73.3 (2008): 387–96.
7.   C. Sinsky, L. Colligan, L. Li, M. Prgomet, S. Reynolds, L. Goeders and G. Blike, 'Allocation of Physician Time in Ambulatory Practice: A Time and Motion Study in 4 Specialties', *Annals of Internal Medicine* 165.11 (2016): 753–60.
8.   T.D. Shanafelt, L.N. Dyrbye, C. Sinsky, O. Hasan, D. Satele, J. Sloan and C.P. West, 'Relationship between Clerical Burden and Characteristics of the Electronic Environment with Physician Burnout and Professional Satisfaction', *Mayo Clinic Proceedings* 91.7 (2016): 836–48.
9.   C. Maslach and M.P. Leiter, 'The Truth about Burnout: How Organizations Cause Personal Stress and What to Do about It', John Wiley & Sons, 2008.

10. https://www.kronos.com/about-us/newsroom/employee-burnout-crisis-study-reveals-big-workplace-challenge-2017

11. E.E. Manlove, 'Multiple Correlates of Burnout in Child Care Workers', *Early Childhood Research Quarterly* 8.4 (1993): 499–518.

12. G. Alarcon, K.J. Eschleman and N.A. Bowling, 'Relationship between Personality Variables and Burnout: A Meta-analysis', *Work and Stress* 23 (2009): 244–63.

13. A.M. Pines, *Burnout: An Existential Perspective* (1993).

14. K.M. Nowack, 'Type A, Hardiness and Psychological Distress', *Journal of Behavioral Medicine* 9.6 (1986): 537–48.

15. G.S. Seibert, K.N. Bauer, R.W. May and F.D. Fincham, 'Emotion Regulation and Academic Underperformance: The Role of School Burnout', *Learning and Individual Differences* 60 (2017): 1–9.

16. K.M. Nowack and A.M. Pentkowski, 'Lifestyle Habits, Substance Use and Predictors of Job Burnout in Professional Working Women', *Work & Stress* 8.1 (1994): 19–35.

17. M. Söderström, K. Jeding, M. Ekstedt, A. Perski and T. Åkerstedt, 'Insufficient Sleep Predicts Clinical Burnout', *Journal of Occupational Health Psychology* 17.2 (2012): 175.

Chapter 4: What Happens If You Don't Act Now

1. I. Savic, 'Structural Changes of the Brain in Relation to Occupational Stress', *Cerebral Cortex* 25 (2015): 1554–64.

2. H. Kim, J. Ji and D. Kao, 'Burnout and Physical Health among Social Workers: A Three-Year Longitudinal Study', *Social Work* 56.3 (2011): 258–68.

3. C.A. Maglione-Garves, L. Kravitz and S. Schneider, 'Cortisol Connection: Tips on Managing Stress and Weight', *ACSM's Health & Fitness Journal* 9.5 (2005): 20–23; Sharon Toker, 'Burnout and Risk of Coronary Heart Disease: A Prospective Study of 8838 Employees, *Psychosomatic Medicine* (2013).

4. S. Jayaratne, W.A. Chess and D.A. Kunkel, 'Burnout: Its Impact on Child Welfare Workers and Their Spouses', *Social Work* 31.1 (1986): 53–59.

5. S.E. Jackson and C. Maslach, 'After-effects of Job-related Stress: Families as Victims', *Journal of Organizational Behavior* 3.1 (1982): 63–77.

6. B.L. Fredrickson, 'The Role of Positive Emotions in Positive Psychology: The Broaden-And-Build Theory of Positive Emotions', *American Psychologist* 56.3 (2001): 218.

7. https://www.hrreview.co.uk/hr-news/wellbeing-news/employee-burnout-a-major-cause-of-absenteeism/52039

8. https://www.cdc.gov/chronicdisease/resources/publications/aag/workplace-health.htm

9. https://www.enrich.org/blog/The-true-cost-of-employee-turnover-financial-wellness-enrich

10. J. Goh, J. Pfeffer and S.A. Zenios, 'The Relationship Between Workplace Stressors and Mortality and Health Costs in the United States'.

11. https://news.gallup.com/businessjournal/162953/tackle-employees-stagnating-engagement.aspx

12. C. Andel, S.L. Davidow, M. Hollander and D.A. Moreno, 'The Economics of Health Care Quality and Medical Errors', *Journal of Health Care Finance* 39.1 (2012): 39.

13. J.S. Wallerstein and J. Lewis, 'The Long-Term Impact of Divorce on Children: A First Report from a 25-Year Study', *Family Court Review* 36.3 (1998): 368–83.

14. http://www.highlandspringgroup.com/press-and-media/group-news/article/34-minutes-the-amount-of-time-the-average-family-gets-to-spend-together-each-day

15. M.A. Milkie, K.M. Nomaguchi and K.E. Denny, 'Does the Amount of Time Mothers Spend with Children or Adolescents Matter?', *Journal of Marriage and Family* 77.2 (2015): 355–72.

16. https://www.cigna.com/newsroom/news-releases/2018/new-cigna-study-reveals-loneliness-at-epidemic-levels-in-america
17. https://www.nytimes.com/2018/01/17/world/europe/uk-britain-loneliness.html

Chapter 5: The Well-being State Pyramid: A Structured Approach to Get Started

1. E. Diener, 'Subjective Well Being', *Psychological Bulletin* 95 (1984): 542–75.
2. H. Naci and J.P. Ioannidis, 'Evaluation of Wellness Determinants and Interventions by Citizen Scientists', *Jama* 314.2 (2015): 121–22.
3. M. Oaten and K. Cheng, 'Improved Self-Control: The Benefits of a Regular Program of Academic Study, *Basic and Applied Psychology* 28: 1–16.

Chapter 6: Don't Be a Victim, Hold Yourself Accountable

1. https://blogs-images.forbes.com/rodgerdeanduncan/files/2018/05/Ladder-of-Accountability.png
2. M.E.P. Seligman, 'Learned Helplessness', *Annual Review of Medicine* 23.1 (1972): 407–12.
3. J. Rodin, 'Aging and Health: Effects of the Sense of Control', *Science* 233.4770 (1986): 1271–76.
4. A. Bandura, 'Self-efficacy: Toward a Unifying Theory of Behavioral Change', *Psychological Review* 84.2 (1977): 191.

Chapter 7: Find Your Purpose

1. https://theenergyproject.com
2. https://hbr.org/1989/09/speed-simplicity-self-confidence-an-interview-with-jack-welch

3. T.D. Shanafelt, C.P. West, J.A. Sloan, P.J. Novotny, G.A. Poland, R. Menaker and L.N. Dyrbye, 'Career Fit and Burnout among Academic Faculty', *Archives of Internal Medicine* 169.10 (2009): 990–95.

4. https://twitter.com/globalcitizenyr/status/1004385453003374592

5. https://craigsroda.com/personal-mission-statement

6. A. Blanchfield, J. Hardy and S. Marcora, 'Non-conscious Visual Cues Related to Affect and Action Alter Perception of Effort and Endurance Performance', *Frontiers in Human Neuroscience* 8 (2014): 967.

7. https://www.beqom.com/blog/jfk-and-the-janitor

8. J.I. Menges, D.V. Tussing, A. Wihler and A.M. Grant, 'When Job Performance Is All Relative: How Family Motivation Energizes Effort and Compensates for Intrinsic Motivation', *Academy of Management Journal* 60.2 (2017): 695–719.

9. W. Liu and J. Aaker, 'The Happiness of Giving: The Time-Ask Effect', *Journal of Consumer Research* 35.3 (2008): 543–57.

10. A.M. Grant and F. Gino, 'A Little Thanks Goes a Long Way: Explaining Why Gratitude Expressions Motivate Prosocial Behavior', *Journal of Personality and Social Psychology* 98.6 (2010): 946.

11. D.R. Van Tongeren, J.D. Green, D.E. Davis, J.N. Hook and T.L. Hulsey, 'Prosociality Enhances Meaning in Life', *Journal of Positive Psychology* 11.3 (2016): 225–36.

12. N. Weinstein and R.M. Ryan, 'When Helping Helps: Autonomous Motivation for Prosocial Behavior and Its Influence on Well-Being for the Helper and Recipient', *Journal of Personality and Social Psychology* 98.2 (2010): 222.

13. S.E. Jackson and C. Maslach, 'After-effects of Job-Related Stress: Families as Victims', *Journal of Organizational Behavior* 3.1 (1982): 63–77.

14. C. Baruch-Feldman, E. Brondolo, D. Ben-Dayan and J. Schwartz, 'Sources of Social Support and Burnout, Job Satisfaction, and Productivity', *Journal of Occupational Health Psychology* 7.1 (2002): 84–93.

Chapter 9: Eat Right for Good Performance

1. https://www.heart.org/en
2. N.J. Nevanperä, L. Hopsu, E. Kuosma, O. Ukkola, J. Uitti and J.H. Laitinen, 'Occupational Burnout, Eating Behavior, and Weight among Working Women', *American Journal of Clinical Nutrition* 95.4 (2012): 934–43.
3. https://www.thedailymeal.com/news/healthy-eating/more-half-americans-skip-breakfast-least-once-week-study-says/081815
4. Y. Ma, E.R. Bertone, E.J. Stanek III, G.W. Reed, J.R. Hebert, N.L. Cohen and I.S. Ockene, 'Association between Eating Patterns and Obesity in a Free-Living US Adult Population', *American Journal of Epidemiology* 158.1 (2003): 85–92.
5. S. Danzigera, J. Levavb and L. Avnaim-Pessoa, 'Extraneous Factors in Judicial Decisions', *PNAS* 108.17 (2011): 6889–92.
6. S.H.A. Holt, H.J. Delargy, C.L. Lawton and J.E. Blundell, 'The Effects of High-Carbohydrate Vs High-Fat Breakfasts on Feelings of Fullness and Alertness, and Subsequent Food Intake', *International Journal of Food Sciences and Nutrition* 50.1 (1999): 13–28.
7. A.P. Smith, 'An Investigation of the Effects of Breakfast Cereals on Alertness, Cognitive Function and Other Aspects of the Reported Well-Being of Children', *Nutritional Neuroscience* 13.5 (2010): 230–36.
8. T.S. Conner, K.L. Brookie, A.C. Richardson and M.A. Polak, 'On Carrots and Curiosity: Eating Fruit and Vegetables Is Associated with Greater Flourishing in Daily Life', *British Journal of Health Psychology* 20.2 (2015): 413–27.

9. https://news.gallup.com/poll/184388/americans-coffee-consumption-steady-few-cut-back.aspx

10. https://www.mayoclinic.org/healthy-lifestyle/nutrition-and-healthy-eating/in-depth/caffeine/art-20045678

11. W. Willett, *Eat, Drink, and Be Healthy: The Harvard Medical School Guide to Healthy Eating* (Simon and Schuster, 2017).

12. G.M. Timmerman and A. Brown, 'The Effect of a Mindful Restaurant Eating Intervention on Weight Management in Women', *Journal of Nutrition Education and Behavior* 44.1 (2012): 22–28.

13. C.H. Jordan, W. Wang, L. Donatoni and B.P. Meier, 'Mindful Eating: Trait and State Mindfulness Predict Healthier Eating Behavior', *Personality and Individual Differences* 68 (2014): 107–11.

14. https://www.cbc.ca/news/canada/british-columbia/jennifer-newman-eating-lunch-with-colleagues-can-boost-productivity-1.3509016

15. K.M. Kniffin, B. Wansink, C.M. Devine and J. Sobal, 'Eating Together At the Firehouse: How Workplace Commensality Relates to the Performance of Firefighters', *Human Performance* 28.4 (2015): 281–306.

16. J.A. Fulkerson, J. Strauss, D. Neumark-Sztainer, M. Story and K. Boutelle, 'Correlates of Psychosocial Well-Being among Overweight Adolescents: The Role of the Family', *Journal of Consulting and Clinical Psychology* 75.1 (2007): 181.

17. E. FitzPatrick, L.S. Edmunds and B.A. Dennison, 'Positive Effects of Family Dinner Are Undone By Television Viewing', *Journal of the American Dietetic Association* 107.4 (2007): 666–71.

18. https://www.theepochtimes.com/puzzled-about-protein-in-your-diet_2499473.html

19. https://hbr.org/2014/10/what-you-eat-affects-your-productivity.

Chapter 10: Get a Good Night's Sleep

1. https://www.sleepfoundation.org/press-release/longer-work-days-leave-americans-nodding-job?utm_source=feedburner&utm_medium=feed&utm_campaign=Feed%3A+nsfalert+%28Newsletter+-+NSF+Alert%29

2. C. Leonard, N. Fanning, J. Attwood and M. Buckley, 'The Effect of Fatigue, Sleep Deprivation and Onerous Working Hours on the Physical and Mental Wellbeing of Pre-Registration House Officers', *Irish Journal of Medical Science* 167.1 (1998): 22.

3. Consensus Conference Panel, N.F. Watson, M.S. Badr, G. Belenky, D.L. Bliwise, O.M. Buxton and C. Kushida, 'Joint Consensus Statement of the American Academy of Sleep Medicine and Sleep Research Society on the Recommended Amount of Sleep for a Healthy Adult: Methodology And Discussion', *Sleep* 38.8 (2015): 1161–83.

4. B.M. Altevogt and H.R. Colten, eds, *Sleep Disorders and Sleep Deprivation: An Unmet Public Health Problem* (National Academies Press, 2006).

5. A. Huffington, *The Sleep Revolution: Transforming Your Life, One Night At a Time* (Harmony, 2016).

6. https://www.sciencedaily.com/releases/2016/11/161130130826.htm

7. M.R. Rosekind, K.B. Gregory, M.M. Mallis, S.L. Brandt, B. Seal and D. Lerner, 'The Cost of Poor Sleep: Workplace Productivity Loss and Associated Costs', *Journal of Occupational and Environmental Medicine* 52.1 (2010): 91–98.

8. M. Söderström, K. Jeding, M. Ekstedt, A. Perski and T. Åkerstedt, 'Insufficient Sleep Predicts Clinical Burnout', *Journal of Occupational Health Psychology* 17.2 (2012): 175.

9. M. Ekstedt, M. Söderström and T. Åkerstedt, 'Sleep Physiology in Recovery from Burnout', *Biological Psychology* 82.3 (2009): 267–73.

10. P. Whitney and J.M. Hinson, 'Measurement of Cognition in Studies of Sleep Deprivation', *Progress in Brain Research* 185 (2010): 37–48.

11. https://medium.com/taking-note/why-a-lack-of-sleep-is-a-productivity-nightmare-8e3dc1fa3d07

12. R. Stickgold and J.M. Ellenbogen, 'Quiet! Sleeping Brain at Work', *Scientific American Mind* 19.4 (2008): 22–29.

13. https://news.gallup.com/poll/181583/getting-sleep-linked-higher.aspx

14. D. Kahneman and A. Deaton, 'High Income Improves Evaluation of Life But Not Emotional Well-Being', *Proceedings of the National Academy of Sciences* 107.38 (2010): 16489–93.

15. https://science.nasa.gov/science-news/science-at-nasa/2005/03jun_naps

16. https://www.sleep.org/articles/sleeping-work-companies-nap-rooms-snooze-friendly-policies

17. J.B. Maas, M.L. Wherry, D.J. Axelrod and B.R. Hogan, *Power Sleep: The Revolutionary Program That Prepares Your Mind for Peak Performance* (Villard, 1998).

18. http://www.sleepfoundation.org/article/how-sleep-works/the-sleep-environment

19. D.S. Black, G.A. O'reilly, R. Olmstead, E.C. Breen and M.R. Irwin, 'Mindfulness Meditation and Improvement in Sleep Quality and Daytime Impairment among Older Adults with Sleep Disturbances: A Randomized Clinical Trial', *JAMA Internal Medicine* 175.4 (2015): 494–501.

20. L.E. Carlson and S.N. Garland, 'Impact of Mindfulness-Based Stress Reduction (Mbsr) on Sleep, Mood, Stress and Fatigue Symptoms in Cancer Outpatients', *International Journal of Behavioral Medicine* 12.4 (2005): 278–85.

Chapter 11: Exercise

1. Y. Yamada, M. Ishizaki and I. Tsuritani, 'Prevention of Weight Gain and Obesity in Occupational Populations: A New Target of Health Promotion Services At Worksites', *Journal of Occupational Health* 44.6 (2002): 373–84.

2. M. Moreau, F. Valente, R. Mak, et al., 'Obesity, Body Fat Distribution and Incidence if Sick Leave in the Belgian Workforce: The Belstress Study', *Int J Obes Relat Metab Disord* 28 (2004): 574–82.

3. W.N. Burton, C.Y. Chen, A.B. Schultz, D.W. Edington, 'The Economic Costs Associated with Body Mass Index in a Workplace', *J Occup Environ Med.* 40 (1998): 786–92.

4. L.A. Tucker, G.M. Friedman, 'Obesity and Absenteeism: An Epidemiologic Study of 10,825 Employed Adults', *Am J Health Promot* 12 (1998): 202–07.

5. F.J. Penedo and J.R. Dahn, 'Exercise and Well-Being: A Review of Mental and Physical Health Benefits Associated with Physical Activity', *Current Opinion in Psychiatry* 18.2 (2005): 189–93.

6. https://www.mayoclinic.org/healthy-lifestyle/fitness/in-depth/exercise/art-20048389

7. C.L. Hogan, J. Mata and L.L. Carstensen, 'Exercise Holds Immediate Benefits for Affect and Cognition in Younger and Older Adults', *Psychology and Aging* 28.2 (2013): 587.

8. L.T. Hoyt, M.G. Craske, S. Mineka and E.K., 'Positive and Negative Affect and Arousal: Cross-Sectional and Longitudinal Associations with Adolescent Cortisol Diurnal Rhythms', *Psychosomatic Medicine* 77.4 (2015): 392.

9. J.A. Blumenthal, M.A. Babyak, K.A. Moore, W.E. Craighead, S. Herman, P. Khatri and P.M. Doraiswamy, 'Effects of Exercise Training on Older Patients with Major Depression', *Archives of Internal Medicine* 159.19 (1999): 2349–56.

10. F. Dimeo, M. Bauer, I. Varahram, G. Proest and U. Halter, 'Benefits from Aerobic Exercise in Patients with Major Depression: A Pilot Study', *British Journal of Sports Medicine* 35.2 (2001): 114–17.

11. A.W. Li and C.A.W. Goldsmith, 'The Effects of Yoga on Anxiety and Stress', *Alternative Medicine Review* 17.1 (2012).

12. A. Malathi and A. Damodaran, 'Stress Due to Exams in Medical Students—Role of Yoga', *Indian J Physiol Pharmacol* 43 (1999) 218–24.

13. J.C. Coulson, J. McKenna and M. Field, 'Exercising at Work and Self-reported Work Performance', *International Journal of Workplace Health Management* 1.3 (2008): 176–97.

14. R.E. Thayer, *The Origin of Everyday Moods: Managing Energy, Tension, and Stress* (Oxford University Press, 1997).

15. M.T. Ballew and A.M. Omoto, 'Absorption: How Nature Experiences Promote Awe and Other Positive Emotions'

Chapter 12: Think Positive

1. https://www.youtube.com/watch?v=eCekUQFG1oU

2. J.R. Andrews-Hanna, R.H. Kaiser, A.E. Turner, A. Reineberg, D. Godinez, S. Dimidjian and M. Banich, 'A Penny for Your Thoughts: Dimensions of Self-Generated Thought Content and Relationships with Individual Differences in Emotional Wellbeing', *Frontiers in Psychology* 4 (2013): 900.

3. B.L. Fredrickson, 'Cultivating Positive Emotions to Optimize Health and Well-Being', *Prevention & Treatment* 3.1 (2000): 1a.

4. J. Strack, P. Lopes, F. Esteves and P. Fernandez-Berrocal, 'Must We Suffer to Succeed? When Anxiety Boosts Motivation and Performance', *Journal of Individual Differences* 38.2 (2017): 113; J. Strack, P.N. Lopes and F. Esteves, 'Will You Thrive Under Pressure or Burn Out? Linking Anxiety

Motivation and Emotional Exhaustion', *Cognition and Emotion* 29.4 (2015): 578–91.

5. Andrea C. Samson; James J. Gross, 'Humour as Emotion Regulation: The Differential Consequences of Negative versus Positive Humour', *Cognition & Emotion* 26.2 (2012): 375–84.

6. C. Eagleson, S. Hayes, A. Mathews, G. Perman and C.R. Hirsch, 'The Power of Positive Thinking: Pathological Worry Is Reduced by Thought Replacement in Generalized Anxiety Disorder', *Behaviour Research and Therapy* 78 (2016): 13–18.

7. A.J. Cuddy, C.A. Wilmuth and D.R. Carney, 'The Benefit of Power Posing Before a High-Stakes Social Evaluation', 2012.

8. P. Briñol, R.E. Petty and B. Wagner, 'Body Posture Effects on Self-Evaluation: A Self-Validation Approach', *European Journal of Social Psychology* 39.6 (2009): 1053–64.

9. D.R. Carney, A.J. Cuddy and A.J. Yap, 'Power Posing: Brief Nonverbal Displays Affect Neuroendocrine Levels and Risk Tolerance', *Psychological Science* 21.10 (2010): 1363–68.

Chapter 13: Practise Mindfulness

1. E.J. Langer, *Mindfulness* (Addison-Wesley/Addison Wesley Longman, 1989).

2. https://hbr.org/2015/12/the-busier-you-are-the-more-you-need-mindfulness

3. M.A. Killingsworth and D.T. Gilbert, 'A Wandering Mind Is an Unhappy Mind', *Science* 330.6006 (2010): 932.

4. S.L. Keng, M.J. Smoski and C.J. Robins, 'Effects of Mindfulness on Psychological Health: A Review of Empirical Studies', *Clinical Psychology Review* 31.6 (2011): 1041–56.

5. S.L. Valk, B.C. Bernhardt, F.M. Trautwein, A. Böckler, P. Kanske, N. Guizard and T. Singer, 'Structural Plasticity of the Social Brain: Differential Change After Socio-Affective

and Cognitive Mental Training', *Science Advances* 3.10 (2017).

6. E.M. Seppälä, J.B. Nitschke, D.L. Tudorascu, A. Hayes, M.R. Goldstein, D.T. Nguyen and R.J. Davidson, 'Breathing-based Meditation Decreases Posttraumatic Stress Disorder Symptoms in US Military Veterans: A Randomized Controlled Longitudinal Study', *Journal of Traumatic Stress* 27.4 (2014): 397–405.

7. https://www.huffpost.com/entry/mindfulness-is-aetna-ceos-prescription-for-success_b_5a4bf577e4b0d86c803c7a1f

8. B.L. Fredrickson, M.A. Cohn, K.A. Coffey, J. Pek and S.M. Finkel, 'Open Hearts Build Lives: Positive Emotions, Induced Through Loving-Kindness Meditation, Build Consequential Personal Resources', *Journal of Personality and Social Psychology* 95.5 (2008): 1045.

Chapter 14: Double Up on friends

1. https://charterforcompassion.org/becoming-compassionate/darwin-revisited-compassion-key-to-our-survival

2. J. Holt-Lunstad, T.B. Smith and J.B. Layton, 'Social Relationships and Mortality Risk: A Meta-Analytic Review', *PLoS Medicine* 7.7 (2010).

3. S.D. Pressman and S. Cohen, 'Does Positive Affect Influence Health?' *Psychological Bulletin* 131 (2005):, 925–71.

4. D. Buettner, *The Blue Zones: 9 Lessons for Living Longer from the People Who've Lived the Longest* (National Geographic Books, 2012).

5. http://www.familiesandwork.org/site/research/reports/dual-centric.pdf

6. G.E. Vaillant, *Aging Well: Surprising Guideposts to a Happier Life from the Landmark Study of Adult Development* (Little, Brown, 2008).

7. R.M. Kaplan and R.G. Kronick, 'Marital Status and Longevity in the United States Population', *Journal of Epidemiology & Community Health* 60.9 (2006): 760–65.

8. J.A. Coan, H.S. Schaefer and R.J. Davidson, 'Lending a Hand: Social Regulation of the Neural Response to Threat', *Psychological Science* 17.12 (2006): 1032–39.

9. S. Achor, *The Happiness Advantage: The Seven Principles of Positive Psychology That Fuel Success and Performance At Work* (Random House, 2011).

10. C. Viswesvaran, J.I. Sanchez and J. Fisher, 'The Role of Social Support in the Process of Work Stress: A Meta-Analysis', *Journal of Vocational Behavior* 54 (1999): 314–34.

11. J.W. Pennebaker, S.D. Barger and J. Tiebout, 'Disclosure of Traumas and Health among Holocaust Survivors', *Psychosomatic Medicine* (1989).

12. B. Rime, B. Mesquita, S. Boca and P. Philippot, 'Beyond the Emotional Event: Six Studies on the Social Sharing of Emotion', *Cognition & Emotion* 5.5–6 (1991): 435–65.

13. B. Brown, *Daring Greatly: How the Courage to Be Vulnerable Transforms the Way We Live, Love, Parent, and Lead* (Penguin, 2015).

Chapter 15: Be Grateful and Give Back

1. R.A. Emmons and M.E. McCullough, 'Counting Blessings versus Burdens: Experimental Studies of Gratitude and Subjective Well-Being', *Journal of Personality and Social Psychology* 84.2 (2003): 377–89.

2. P.C. Watkins, K. Woodward, T. Stone and R.L. Kolts, 'Gratitude and Happiness: Development of a Measure of Gratitude, and Relationships with Subjective Well-Being', *Social Behavior and Personality* 31.5 (2003): 431.

3. M.E. Seligman, T.A. Steen, N. Park and C. Peterson, 'Positive Psychology Progress: Empirical Validation of Interventions', *American Psychologist* 60.5 (2005): 410.

4. E.W. Dunn, L.B. Aknin and M.I. Norton, 'Spending Money on Others Promotes Happiness', *Science* 319.5870 (2008): 1687–88.

5. A.V. Whillans, E.W. Dunn, G.M. Sandstrom, S.S. Dickerson and K.M. Madden, 'Is Spending Money on Others Good for Your Heart? *Health Psychology* 35.6 (2016): 574.

6. https://greatergood.berkeley.edu/article/item/tips_for_keeping_a_gratitude_journal

7. https://www.robinsharma.com/article/how-to-keep-a-journal

8. M. Ricard, *Altruism: The Power of Compassion to Change Yourself and the World* (Hachette UK, 2015).

Chapter 16: Smile and Laugh

1. T.L. Kraft and S.D. Pressman, 'Grin and Bear It: The Influence of Manipulated Facial Expression on the Stress Response', *Psychological Science* 23.11 (2012): 1372–78.

2. L. Harker and D. Keltner, 'Expressions of Positive Emotion in Women's College Yearbook Pictures and Their Relationship to Personality and Life Outcomes across Adulthood', *Journal of Personality and Social Psychology* 80.1 (2001): 112.

3. J.P. Seder and S. Oishi, 'Intensity of Smiling in Facebook Photos Predicts Future Life Satisfaction', *Social Psychological and Personality Science* 3.4 (2012): 407–13.

4. E. Finzi and E. Wasserman, 'Treatment of Depression with Botulinum Toxin A: A Case Series' *Dermatologic Surgery* 32.5 (2006): 645–50.

5. M.B. Lewis and P.J. Bowler, 'Botulinum Toxin Cosmetic Therapy Correlates with a More Positive Mood', *Journal of Cosmetic Dermatology* 8.1 (2009): 24–26.

6. M. Sonnby–Borgström, 'Automatic Mimicry Reactions as Related to Differences in Emotional Empathy', *Scandinavian Journal of Psychology* 43 (2002): 433–43.

7.   R. Gutman, *Smile: The Astonishing Powers of a Simple Act* (TED Books, 2011).

8.   https://www.firstcoastnews.com/article/news/health/laughing-makes-your-brain-work-better-new-study-finds/271190115

9.   A. Deshpande and V. Verma, 'Effect of Laughter Therapy on Happiness and Life Satisfaction among Elderly', *Indian Journal of Positive Psychology* 4.1 (2013): 153–63.

10. M.J. Balick and R. Lee, 'The Role of Laughter In Traditional Medicine and Its Relevance to the Clinical Setting: Healing With Ha!', 2003.

Chapter 17: Work Smart: The Ten Pillars for Building Efficiencies

1.   D.H. Pink, *When: The Scientific Secrets of Perfect Timing* (Penguin Press, 2019).

2.   https://hbr.org/2017/04/employee-burnout-is-a-problem-with-the-company-not-the-person

3.   S.T. Iqbal and E. Horvitz, 'Disruption and Recovery of Computing Tasks: Field Study, Analysis, and Directions', *CHI* 7 (2007): 677–86.

4.   R.C. Pozen, *Extreme Productivity: Boost Your Results, Reduce Your Hours* (Harper Business, 2012).

5.   A. Ariga and A. Lleras, 'Brief and Rare Mental "Breaks" Keep You Focused: Deactivation and Reactivation of Task Goals Preempt Vigilance Decrements', *Cognition* 118.3 (2011): 439–43.

6.   N. Kleitman, *Sleep and Wakefulness* (Chicago: University of Chicago Press, 1963).

7.   https://www.inc.com/jessica-stillman/the-magic-numbers-for-maximum-productivity-52-and-17.html

8.   E.L. Rossi and D. Nimmons, *The 20 Minute Break* (Los Angeles: Jeremy P. Tarcher, 1991).

9. S. Mann and R. Cadman, 'Does Being Bored Make Us More Creative?' *Creativity Research Journal* 26.2 (2014): 165–73.

10. https://www.k-state.edu/media/newsreleases/jul14/smartphone7714.html

11. A.F. Ward, K. Duke, A. Gneezy and M.W. Bos, 'Brain Drain: The Mere Presence of One's Own Smartphone Reduces Available Cognitive Capacity', *Journal of the Association for Consumer Research* 2.2 (2017): 140–54.

12. J.H. Aranda and S. Baig, 'Toward JOMO: The Joy of Missing Out and the Freedom of Disconnecting', *Proceedings of the 20th International Conference on Human–Computer Interaction with Mobile Devices and Services* (2018): 19.

13. J. De Bloom, S.A. Geurts and M.A. Kompier, 'Vacation (After-) Effects on Employee Health and Well-Being, and the Role of Vacation Activities, Experiences and Sleep', *Journal of Happiness Studies* 14.2 (2013): 613–33.

14. https://www.kornferry.com/press/15179

15. M. Westman and D. Etzion, 'The Impact of Vacation and Job Stress on Burnout and Absenteeism', *Psychology & Health* 16.5 (2001): 595–606.

16. R.A. Atchley, D.L. Strayer and P. Atchley, 'Creativity in the Wild: Improving Creative Reasoning Through Immersion in Natural Settings', *PloS One* 7.12 (2012): e51474.

17. S. Sonnentag, 'Psychological Detachment from Work During Leisure Time: The Benefits of Mentally Disengaging from Work', *Current Directions in Psychological Science* 21.2 (2012): 114–18.

18. https://www.bravotv.com/blogs/if-you-want-a-promotion-or-a-raise-you-need-to-take-not-skip-vacation

Chapter 18: Change Management: Consistent Actions lead to Change

1. https://www.youtube.com/watch?v=hiiEeMN7vbQ

2.   R.F. Baumeister, E. Bratslavsky and M. Muraven, *Ego Depletion: Is the Active Self a Limited Resource? Self-Regulation and Self-Control* (Routledge, 2018), pp. 24–52.

Chapter 19: Create Humane Organizations and Societies

1.   K.J. Schneider, J.F. Pierson and J.F. Bugental, eds, *The Handbook of Humanistic Psychology: Theory, Research, and Practice* (Sage Publications, 2014).

2.   K. Cameron, *Positive Leadership: Strategies for Extraordinary Performance* (Berrett-Koehler Publishers, 2012).

3.   M. Worline and J.E. Dutton, *Awakening Compassion at Work: The Quiet Power That Elevates People and Organizations* (Berrett-Koehler Publishers, 2017).

4.   S.G. Barsade and O.A. O'Neill, 'What's Love Got to Do with It? A Longitudinal Study of the Culture of Companionate Love and Employee and Client Outcomes in a Long-Term Care Setting', *Administrative Science Quarterly* 59.4 (2014): 551–98.

5.   L.T. Thomas and D.C. Ganster, 'Impact of Family-Supportive Work Variables on Work-Family Conflict and Strain: A Control Perspective', *Journal of Applied Psychology* 80.1 (1995): 6.

6.   https://www.nytimes.com/2011/12/24/business/volkswagen-curbs-company-e-mail-in-off-hours.html

7.   https://www.fastcompany.com/3034699/a-brilliant-strategy-to-avoid-checking-emails-on-vacation-auto-delete-them

8.   A. Nyberg, P. Bernin and T. Theorell, *The Impact of Leadership on the Health of Subordinates* (Stockholm: National Institute for Working Life [Arbetslivsinstitutet], 2005).

9.   https://theenergyproject.com/why-you-hate-work-2/

10.   M. Vianello, E.M. Galliani and J. Haidt, 'Elevation at Work: The Effects of Leaders' Moral Excellence', *The Journal of Positive Psychology* 5.5 (2010): 390–411.

11. N.A. Christakis and J.H. Fowler, *Connected: The Surprising Power of Our Social Networks and How They Shape Our Lives* (Little, Brown, 2009).

12. https://www.workforce.com/2013/02/20/part-of-boston-consulting-groups-success-comes-from-looking-out-for-its-workers/

13. E.L. Kelly, P. Moen, J.M. Oakes, W. Fan, C. Okechukwu, K.D. Davis and F. Mierzwa, 'Changing Work and Work-Family Conflict: Evidence from the Work, Family, and Health Network', *American Sociological Review* 79.3 (2014): 485–516.

14. K.D. Davis, K.M. Lawson, D.M. Almeida, E.L. Kelly, R.B. King, L. Hammer and S.M. McHale, 'Parents' Daily Time with Their Children: A Workplace Intervention', *Pediatrics* 135.5 (2015): 875.

15. https://money.cnn.com/2017/01/02/technology/france-office-email-workers-law/index.html

16. https://www.internationallaborlaw.com/2019/01/29/more-countries-consider-implementing-a-right-to-disconnect/

17. https://www.upi.com/Top_News/World-News/2018/10/02/South-Koreans-work-fewer-hours-since-adoption-of-52-hour-work-week/8951538465944/

18. https://www.businessinsider.com/new-york-city-after-hours-work-email-2018-3

19. https://www.theguardian.com/world/2018/oct/02/no-downside-new-zealand-firm-adopts-four-day-week-after-successful-trial

20. https://qz.com/504623/swedish-social-experiment-highlights-the-benefits-of-a-six-hour-work-day

21. P. Best, R. Manktelow and B. Taylor, 'Online Communication, Social Media and Adolescent Wellbeing: A Systematic Narrative Review', *Children and Youth Services Review* 41 (2014): 27–36.

22. P. Sahlberg, *Finnish Lessons* (Teachers College Press, 2011).

23. https://www.straitstimes.com/singapore/education/fewer-exams-for-students-less-emphasis-on-grades

24. http://uaap.mit.edu/first-year-mit/first-year-academics/
    first-year-academics-first-year-credit-limits-grading/credit-
    limits-grading-first-year-grading-policies
25. https://www.npr.org/2018/07/28/632761402/to-focus-
    on-students-emotional-well-being-india-tries-happiness-
    classes
26. M.T. Greenberg and A.R. Harris, 'Nurturing Mindfulness
    in Children and Youth: Current State of Research', *Child
    Development Perspectives* 6.2 (2012): 161–66.

Chapter 20: Prepare Your Children to Thrive in a Dog-eat-dog World

1. https://www.apa.org/news/press/releases/2009/11/stress
2. R.P. Ang and V.S. Huan, 'Relationship between Academic
    Stress And Suicidal Ideation: Testing For Depression As A
    Mediator Using Multiple Regression', *Child Psychiatry and
    Human Development* 37.2 (2006): 133.
3. A. Aypay, 'Elementary School Student Burnout Scale for
    Grades 6-8: A Study of Validity and Reliability', *Educational
    Sciences: Theory and Practice* 11.2 (2011): 520–27.
4. W.B. Schaufeli, M. Salanova, V. González-Romá and A.B.
    Bakker, 'The Measurement of Engagement and Burnout:
    A Two Sample Confirmatory Factor Analytic Approach',
    Journal of Happiness Studies 3.1 (2002): 71–92.
5. L.N. Dyrbye, C.P. West, D. Satele, S. Boone, L. Tan, J. Sloan
    and T.D. Shanafelt, 'Burnout Among US Medical Students,
    Residents, and Early Career Physicians Relative to the General
    US Population', *Academic Medicine* 89.3 (2014): 443–51.
6. Academy of Finland, 'School Burnout among Adolescents
    Shows Correlation with Parental Work Burnout', *ScienceDaily*
    (January 2010).
7. https://hms.harvard.edu/news/college-stress

8. L.N. Dyrbye, M.R. Thomas, D.V. Power, S. Durning, C. Moutier, F.S. Massie and T.D. Shanafelt, 'Burnout and Serious Thoughts of Dropping Out of Medical School: A Multi-Institutional Study', *Academic Medicine* 85.1 (2010): 94–102.

9. M.E. Eisenberg, R.E. Olson, D. Neumark-Sztainer, M. Story and L.H. Bearinger, 'Correlations between Family Meals and Psychosocial Well-Being among Adolescents', *Archives of Pediatrics & Adolescent Medicine* 158.8 (2004): 792–96.

10. K. Cripps and B. Zyromski, 'Adolescents' Psychological Well-Being and Perceived Parental Involvement: Implications for Parental Involvement in Middle Schools', *RMLE Online* 33.4 (2009): 1–13.

11. E. Galinsky, *Ask the Children: What America's Children Really Think About Working Parents* (William Morrow and Company, 1999).

12. S. Achor, *The Happiness Advantage: The Seven Principles of Positive Psychology That Fuel Success and Performance At Work* (Random House, 2011).

13. S.R. Jacobs and D. Dodd, 'Student Burnout As a Function of Personality, Social Support, and Workload', *Journal of College Student Development* 44.3 (2003): 291–303.

14. https://theconversation.com/how-parents-and-teens-can-reduce-the-impact-of-social-media-on-youth-well-being-87619

15. K.K. Murdock, M. Horissian and C. Crichlow-Ball, 'Emerging Adults' Text Message Use and Sleep Characteristics: A Multimethod, Naturalistic Study', *Behavioral Sleep Medicine* 15.3 (2017): 228–41.

16. K. Salmela-Aro, N. Kiuru, M. Pietikäinen and J. Jokela, 'Does School Matter? The Role of School Context in Adolescents' School-Related Burnout', *European Psychologist* 13.1 (2008): 12–23.

17. https://blog.edmodo.com/2017/07/14/the-global-search-for-education-new-study-shows-student-well-being-is-in-serious-decline

18. P.S. Chu, D.A. Saucier and E. Hafner, 'Meta-analysis of the Relationships between Social Support and Well-Being in Children and Adolescents', *Journal of Social and Clinical Psychology* 29.6 (2010): 624–45.